अ

Let noble

BHAVAN'S BOOK UNIVERSITY

WHO IS WHO IN THE Ramayana

by

Subash Mazumdar

BHAVAN'S BOOK UNIVERSITY

WHO IS WHO IN THE Ramayana

SUBASH MAZUMDAR

2024

BHARATIYA VIDYA BHAVAN
Kulapati K. M. Munshi Marg
Mumbai - 400007

First Edition : *2024*

Price : ₹ 315/-

Typesetting by Samir Parekh
at Creative Page Setters

PRINTED IN INDIA

By Nilesh Parekh, Paras Prints, at Gala 32, Singh Indu. Estate-3, 1st floor, Ram Mandir Road, Goregaon, Mumbai - 400104 and Published by P. V. Sankarankutty, Director, *for* Bharatiya Vidya Bhavan, K.M. Munshi Marg, Mumbai - 400007. E-mail : bhavan@bhavans.info - Website : http://www.bhavans.info

To Anjani, my wife

I know you didn't write
a word of this but
without you I
wouldn't have either.

Subash

KULAPATI'S PREFACE

The Bharatiya Vidya Bhavan—that Institute of Indian Culture in Mumbai—needed a Book University, a series of books which, if read, would serve the purpose of providing higher education. Particular emphasis, however, was to be put on such literature as revealed the deeper impulsions of India. As a first step, it was decided to bring out in English 100 books, 50 of which were to be taken in hand, almost at once.

It is our intention to publish the books we select, not only in English but also in the following Indian languages: Hindi, Bengali, Gujarati, Marathi, Tamil, Telugu, Kannada and Malayalam.

This scheme, involving the publication of 900 volumes, requires ample funds and an all-India organisation. The Bhavan is exerting its utmost to supply them.

The objectives for which the Bhavan stands are the reintegration of Indian culture in the light of modern knowledge and to suit our present-day needs and the resuscitation of its fundamental values in their pristine vigour.

Let me make our goal more explicit:

We seek the dignity of man, which necessarily implies the creation of social conditions which would allow him freedom to evolve along the lines of his own temperament and capacities; we seek the harmony of individual efforts and social relations, not in any makeshift way, but within the framework of the Moral Order; we seek the creative art of life, by the alchemy of which human limitations are progressively transmuted, so that man may become the instrument of God, and is able to see Him in all and all in Him.

The world, we feel, is too much with us. Nothing would uplift or inspire us so much as the beauty and aspiration which such books can teach.

In this *series*, therefore, the literature of India, ancient and modern, will be published in a form easily accessible to all. Books in other literatures of the world, if they illustrate the principles we stand for, will also be included.

This common pool of literature, it is hoped, will enable the reader, eastern or western, to understand and appreciate currents of world thought, as also the movements of the mind in India, which, though they flow through different linguistic channels, have a common urge and aspiration.

Fittingly, the Book University's first venture is the *Mahabharata*, summarised by one of the greatest living Indians, C. Rajagopalachari; the second work is on a section of it, the *Gita* by H.V.Divatia, an eminent jurist and student of philosophy. Centuries ago, it was proclaimed of the *Mahabharata*: "What is not in it, is nowhere." After twenty-five centuries, we can use the same words about it. He who knows it not, knows not the heights and depths of the soul; he misses the trials and tragedy and the beauty and grandeur of life.

The *Mahabharata* is not a mere epic: it is a romance, telling the tale of heroic men and women and of some who were divine; it is a whole literature in itself, containing a code of life, a philosophy of social and ethical relations, and speculative thought on human problems that is hard to rival: but, above all, it has for its core the *Gita,* which is, as the world is beginning to find out, the noblest of scriptures and the grandest of sagas in which the climax is reached in the wondrous Apocalypse in the Eleventh Canto.

Through such books alone the harmonies underlying true culture, I am convinced, will one day reconcile the disorders of modern life.

I thank all those who have helped to make this new branch of the Bhavan's activity successful.

New Delhi

1, Queen Victoria Road,

October 3, 1951

PUBLISHER'S NOTE

Kulapati K. M. Munshi, calling Shri Ramachandra as an 'artist of life in history and mythology', wrote of Him that He was inspired by the permanent values of Indian culture. Munshiji made it his life's mission to propagate these values through the Bharatiya Vidya Bhavan and his speeches and writings. He found the two epics, the *Ramayana* and the *Mahabharata,* as the reservoirs of these values, the foremost of which were Dharma and Satya; they had their origin in the Vedic Rta.

Perhaps, taking the cue from Thomas Carlyle (1795-1881), the eminent Victorian writer who defined a University as 'a collection of books', Munshiji set up a Book University to bring out initially 100 works that would help disseminate the values of our religio-ethical culture. The first to be brought out was the *'Mahabharata'* of C. Rajagopalachari (1878-1972), patriot and writer, and the first Indian Governor-General.

Rama's story is the theme of at least over thirty books published so far by us. Rajaji's *Ramayana* tops the list and it has set up a record of sales—more than fifteen lakh copies. The other distinguished writers on the subject are: Smt. Kamala Subramaniam, Dr. J. K. Trika, Kum. P. C. Dharma, N. S. Mani, Mathuram Bhoothalingam, (Justice) N. Chandrasekhara Iyer, Smt. Janaki Ramachandran, V. V. S. Iyer, H. V. Hande, Sudha Mazumdar, H. H. Jagadguru Sankaracharya Sri Bharatikrishna Tirtha, Sant Shri Morari Bapu, P. N. Murthy, L. Swaminathan, R. K. Sarma, P. Sankaranarayanan and S. L. N. Simha.

The Bhavan achieved overwhelming success by publishing *Ramayana* & *Mahabharata*. The two bestsellers bring Valmiki and Vyasa closer to those who have no access to their unrivalled epics. The Ramayana and the Mahabharata bind our people as one community despite differences of caste and language that seemingly divide them. These books figure in the list of 70 iconic publications of post-independence India drawn up by 'The Hindustan Times'.

It is in the fitness of things that Subash Mazumdar's *'Who is Who in the Ramayana'* giving in brief the role of the main characters and others who figure in the epic is being published.

Subashji is no stranger to the Bhavan. We have already published three of his books including *(i) Who is Who in the Mahabharata, (ii) Mahabharata is Believable* and *(iii) Tales from Puranas.*

An international civilian who was associated with U.N., it is indeed admirable that Subashji could also devote much time to the study of the two great epics of India's ancient and sacred literature. That he shared his study and knowledge with his family members speaks volumes about his interest in our culture.

A melancholy interest is attached to this publication. Subashji passed away in 2019 when he was 90. The manuscript was incomplete in some respects. We have taken the liberty to add or amend wherever necessary while preparing this work for the press. Here is a handy reference book on the *Ramayana*. A timely one, too, considering the enthusiastic celebrations of the consecration of the Sri Rama idol at the magnificent temple in Ayodhya on 22nd January 2024.

Mumbai

1st July 2024 BHARATIYA VIDYA BHAVAN

A

Ahalya

A very beautiful maiden created by Brahma and given in marriage to Gautama rishi. Once Indra, in a fit of passion, assumed the form of Gautama rishi and approached her when she was alone. Ahalya, though aware of the deceit, did not resist Indra's advances. After making love with Ahalya, Indra tried to escape from the ashrama but was confronted by Gautama. The great rishi then cursed Ahalya saying that she would lose all her beauty and virtues and lead a solitary life in the jungle unseen by anyone. Later, he relented a little and added that she would be restored to her original form when she set her eyes on Rama.

This episode was narrated to Rama and Lakshmana by Vishvamitra when they were passing by Gautama rishi's uninhabitated ashrama on their way from Vaishali to Mithila. As Rama entered this ashrama, Ahalya saw him and regained her original form and purity. Thus blessed by Rama she lived happily with Gautama rishi for long.

Aja

Father of King Dasharatha and descendent of the illustrious solar dynasty of Kings such as Mandhata, Harishchandra, Sagara, Raghu, etc.

Ajamukhi

A wicked rakshasi who, along with her companions, wanted to kill Seeta in Ashokavana and then eat her.

Akampana

Ravana's uncle.

Brother of Ravana's mother Kaikasi and a mighty rakshasa. When Ravana sent a band of rakshasas against Rama to avenge the disfigurement of his sister Surpanakha in Dandakaranya, Akampana alone remained alive to describe the strength and valour of Rama and Lakshmana. As Rama could not be killed in any manner, he suggested that Seeta be kidnapped so that Rama would die of grief and sorrow. He fought fiercely in the great battle of Lanka and died at the hands of Hanuman.

Akopa

One of the several ministers of King Dasharatha of Ayodhya.

Akshakumara

One of the sons of Ravana. After crossing the ocean and locating Seeta in Ashokavatika, Hanuman decided to instill fear in the hearts of the rakshasa warriors. He destroyed the forest and killcd a number of rakshasa chiefs who came to capture him. It was then that Ravana sent Akshakumara to get hold of Hanuman. He was killed by Hanuman catching hold of him by the legs and throwing him on the ground after swinging him round and round.

Alambusha

An apsara who married Ikshvaku, the ancestor of Rama and founder of the dynasty. Ikshvaku's son was Vishala. The story of Vishala's ancestors and successors was told by Vishvamitra to Rama and Lakshmana as they passed through the Vishala territory. Vishvamitra told them also the origin of the seven winds–the Marutas–including Vayu. Vishvamitra said that the then ruler of Vishala was King Sumati. He was the son of the celebrated Kakutstha, the illustrions ancestor of Rama. King Sumati entertained the three as his guests for a night. The next day the party reached Mithila; Rama redeemed Ahalya on the way.

Alarka

A virtuous King of ancient times who once promised to give to a visiting brahmana whatever he asked for. The brahmana, being blind, asked for the King's eyes which Alarka gave him readily and kept his word. This episode was related by Kaikeyi to Dasharatha in order to urge him to keep his word and fulfill her wishes in accordance with the promise he had made to her.

Ambarisha

A King of ancient times who, having lost his sacrificial beast, purchased Ruchik rishi's son Shunashepa to perform the sacrifice. But Vishvamitra, with his power of penance, saved the life of the boy and at the same time helped King Ambarisha to complete his yagna. This anecdote, illustrating the great power of Vishvamitra, was related to King Janaka by his chief priest Shatananda.

Anala

One of the four rakshasas who accompanied Vibhishana when the latter abandoned Ravana and sought Rama's friendship. When the vanara army crossed the ocean and arrived at the door-step of Lanka, Anala, assuming the form of a bird, flew over Lanka and reported to Vibhishana the strength and deployment of the rakshasa army. Vibhishana in turn passed on the vital information to Rama. Anala, the son of Mali, was a cousin of Ravana's mother Kaikasi.

Ananga

This vanara took part in the southern expedition led by prince Angada when King Sugreeva decided to send his forces in all directions in search of Seeta.

Anaranya

An early King of Ayodhya belonging to the Ikshvaku dynasty. Ravana defeated his army and threw the King on the ground. Just before being killed, the King pronounced a curse that an illustrious descendent, by name Rama, would kill him.

Anasuya

Wife of Atri rishi was renowned for her piety and virtue. Rama, Lakshmana and Seeta visited her during their period of banishment in the forest. In addition to blessing Seeta, she derived much joy by adorning her with jewels and a garland of never-fading flowers.

Andhakasura

In ancient times this wicked demon interrupted Shweta rishi's penance. He was killed by Shankara. In this same manner Rama killed Ravana's younger brother Khara. Khara was prompted to attack Rama and Lakshmana by his sister Surpanakha who had been disfigured by Lakshmana.

Angada

Valiant son of vanar King Vali and Queen Tara. Vali before his death directed Angada to give his fullest loyalty to his uncle Sugreeva who was to be crowned as the new King of Kishkindha. Angada was then named as the crown prince.

When Sugreeva decided to send his vanar forces in all directions to search for Seeta, Angada was placed in charge of the expedition that went south. His forces, having had an enjoyable time in the enchanting cave of Suprabha, could not obtain any information about Seeta within the stipulated period of thirty days. Angada was afraid that he would be killed by Sugreeva if he reported failure of his mission. However, Hanuman encouraged him to persevere and helped eventually to end the mission with success.

When the vanar forces crossed the ocean and surrounded Lanka and fighting was about to start, Rama sent Angada as an envoy to warn Ravana that he would soon be destroyed unless he surrendered and arranged the safe return of Seeta. Angada carried out this difficult task. When Ravana refused and wanted to arrest Angada, the latter escaped after destroying parts of Ravana's palace and instilling fear in the minds of the rakshasas.

During the battle Angada fought with extreme bravery, leading repeated charges against the mighty rakshasas and in single combat, he killed rakshasa leaders like Narantaka, Vajradamshtra and Mahaparshva.

Angada attended the coronation of Rama in Ayodhya. Much later when Sugreeva decided to give up his worldly life, Angada became the King of Kishkindha.

Angada

Elder of the two sons of Lakshmana/Urmila, the other being Chandraketu. Towards the end of Rama's life Angada was settled as the King of Karupatha. (Uttara Kanda)

Angaraka

Another name for rakshasi Simhika who lived in the ocean surrounding Lanka and who protected Ravana. She was killed by Hanuman.

Anjana

Mother of Hanuman. She was an apsara called Punjikasthala who, because of the curse of a rishi, had taken the form of a maid in the household of a vanara called Kunjara who eventually regarded her as his daughter. In due course, she married vanara Kesari, the King of Sumeru. Once Pavanadevata (Vayu, Marutta) got enamoured of her and embraced her. Even though Anjana had not deviated from her single-minded devotion to her husband, this divine experience, (mental union) caused her to give birth to Hanuman, also called Pavanaputra.

Anshuman

The story of how Anshuman succeeded in retrieving the ceremonial horse of his grandfather Sagara, an illustrious King of the early Ikshvaku dynasty, was related by Vishvamitra to Rama and Lakshmana when they were on their way to Mithila.

Anurada

In ancient times Anurada had, through trickery, kidnapped Indra's consort Shachidevi and was killed by Indra. This was related by Rama to Sugreeva to drive home the point that Ravana too would be killed in the same manner.

Araja

Daughter of Shukracharya. Once King Danda, out on a hunt, seeing this maiden of uncommon beauty, had a sudden urge to possess her. Araja, however, warned him to seek her father's consent before touching her. King Danda, however, possessed her against her will. When Shukracharya came to know this he cursed that the King's entire country of Dandaka would be rendered lifeless by a duststorm and that not even a bird or an animal would be able to live in the forest. This territory then came to be known as Dandakaranya. It was in this forest that Agastya rishi related this history to Rama just before the latter was to perform the ashwamedha yagna.

Archimalya

Son of Marichi. This mighty vanara formed a part of the team sent by Sugreeva in search of Seeta towards west under the leadership of Sushena.

Archishaman

Along with his brother Archimalya, he too was in the vanara expedition led by Sushena which went westward to look for Seeta.

Arishtanemi

Father of King Sagara's wife, Sumati. He was a descendent of Kashyapa.

Arjuna

A King of the Haihaya dynasty ruling over the city of Mahishmati. Once this mighty King was sporting in river Narmada, with his women. He stopped the flow of the river with his numerous hands. Water overflowed the banks and swept away the flowers which had been collected by the great Ravana for his worship of Shiva. In great anger Ravana attacked Arjuna but, after a prolonged fight, Arjuna defeated Ravana and captured him. It was only at the pleading of Pulastya that Ravana was released. This episode was narrated by Agastya rishi to Rama to illustrate that there were mightier warriors than Ravana. Agastya also described the strength of Hanuman.

Aruna

Son of Vinata – said to be the progenitor of all birds. Father of Jatayu and Sampati–husband of Shyeni.

Arundhati

Consort of Vasishtha.

Asamanja

Son of King Sagara and Queen Keshini. Because of his cruelty towards the subjects, specially children, he was expelled from the Kingdom. His son Anshuman continued the royal lineage. This early history was related by Vishvamitra to young Rama and Lakshmana when they were on their way to Mithila.

Ashaniprabha

A rakshasa who fought with vanara Dvivida at the very beginning of the battle of Lanka.

Ashokanandana

One of the four messengers (the other three being Jayanta, Siddharta and Vijaya) sent by Vasishtha to Kekaya to recall Bharata and Shatrughna from their maternal uncle's place after Rama had left Ayodhya for the forest and King Dasharatha had died of sorrow. The messengers were asked to tell Bharata that his presence was urgently needed in Ayodhya.

Ashvapati

Father of Kaikeyi.

Asurtaraja

One of the four sons of King Kusha of ancient times and his Queen Vaidarbhi (the other three were Kushamba, Kushanabha and Vasu). This early history was related by Vishvamitra to Rama and Lakshmana when they were passing through the country settled by Vasu's descendents, while on their way to Mithila.

Atikaya

Valiant son of Ravana and Queen Dhanyamali. By pleasing Brahma by severe penances, he had obtained some boons and weapons. After the death of his uncle, Kumbhakarna, at the hands of Rama, he entered the battle along with his brothers. He fought bravely and skilfully but was finally beheaded by Lakshmana.

Atri

Rama, Lakshmana and Seeta received the blessings of this great rishi when they passed through his hermitage on their way from Chitrakuta to Dandaka forest. Atri rishi's wife Ansuya then gave divine garments and jewellery to Seeta in appreciation of her virtuous qualities.

Avindhya

This aged rakshasa warned Ravana that the complete destruction of the rakshasa race was inevitable if Seeta was not returned to Rama. But this advice was not acceptable to Ravana.

Ayomukhi

After witnessing the death of Jatayu, when Rama and Lakshmana were proceeding in the forest in search of Seeta, they encountered this fierce and ugly rakshasi. She caught hold of Lakshmana saying that she had fallen in love with him and that he should enjoy her company. Lakshmana, in revulsion, cut off her breasts, nose and ears and made her flee from the place.

B

Bali

A great demon King who had conquered the three worlds and overpowered the devas. At his yagna Vishnu, in his vamana avatara, assumed the form of a brahmana boy and requested three paces of land from the King. When Bali consented, Vishnu assumed a gigantic size and covered the entire universe in two paces. As no more land was left for the third pace, Bali offered his head; Vishnu put his foot on the King's head and pushed him down into the nether world. This episode of early history was related by rishi Vishvamitra to Rama when they were passing by the hermitage known as Siddhashrama, where Vishnu in earlier times had undertaken austerities.

Bhageeratha

Grandson of King Anshuman of Ayodhya and an ancestor of Rama. After pleasing both Brahma and Mahadeva, he succeeded in persuading river Ganga to come down to earth and flow over the ashes of his ancestors who were burnt by Kapila rishi. Thus he accomplished an extremely difficult task by his relentlees efforts (Bhageerata-Prayatna) and enabled his ancestors to achieve salvation.

Bhanumana

King of Kosala who was an honoured guest at the Ashwamedha yagna performed by King Dasharatha.

Bharadwaja

Disciple of sage Vasishtha. It was at this rishi's ashrama that Rama, Lakshmana and Seeta spent a night during their early days of banishment to the forest soon after Bharata made his unsuccessful attempt to persuade Rama to return to Ayodhya. Bharadwaja rishi then indicated a spot where Rama, Lakshmana and Seeta could build their hut and live in peace.

Later, when Bharata went to Bharadwaja's ashrama in search of Rama, the sage provided sumptuous meals, accommodation and entertainment to the entire army of Bharata. Finally, he showed Bharata the way to Chitrakuta ashrama of Rama.

Bharadwaja

Father of Vishrava's wife Devavarnini and grandfather of Kubera.

Bharata

Righteous younger brother of Rama–son of King Dasharatha and Queen Kaikeyi. He married

Mandavi, daughter of King Janaka's younger brother Kushadhwaja. By her he had two sons, Taksha and Pushkala.

Before Rama's proposed coronation as the Crown Prince of Ayodhya, Bharata was away on a short visit to his maternal uncle. Upon his return he learnt that his father King Dasharatha had died pining for his beloved son Rama whom he had been compelled to send away as an exile to the forest for fourteen years in order to keep his promise given earlier to Queen Kaikeyi. He was shocked and berated and blamed his mother Kaikeyi for her greed. He swore that he would never occupy the throne of Ayodhya which rightly belonged to Rama.

After performing the funeral rites of his father, Bharata set out for the forest, accompanied by priests and members of the grieving royal family to persuade Rama to return to Ayodhya and occupy the throne rightfully belonging to Rama. But Rama refused saying that he was duty-bound to honour the words of his father. Bharata then obtained Rama's wooden sandals saying that he would keep them on the throne as a symbol of authority and attend to royal affairs in the name of his elder brother. He then returned to Ayodhya and set up an ashrama at Nandigrama on the outskirts of Ayodhya where he built a temple and installed Rama's sandals. He gave up his royal attire and for fourteen years wore only the modest clothes of a sanyasi and lived on fruits, berries and other forest pickings. Thus passed full fourteen years during which he presided over state affairs as a regent of Rama.

At the end of fourteen years, after Rama's return to Ayodhya, Bharata was made the Crown Prince. Once Rama received a call for help from Kaikeyi's brother who was attacked by gandharvas. Under Bharata's leadership the Ayodhya army vanquished the gandharvas. Bharata then installed his son Taksha as the King of Takshila and Pushkala as the King of Pushkalavata.

At the end of a long and illustrious reign, after Rama had given up his earthly existence, Bharata passed away at the pilgrimage centre of Gopratararatirtha.

Bhaskara

One of the commanders of Ravana's army. Along with Durgharsha, Pradhasa, Virupaksha and Yupaksha he was ordered to confront Hanuman who had caused much havoc in Lanka. He was killed in battle by Hanuman.

Bhaya

A sister of Yama.

Bhrugu

Rishi who told King Sagara that one of his two wives would have a son who would continue the family lineage while the other wife would have sixty thousand brave sons.

Brahmadatta

Manasaputra of Chulee rishi who had produced him out of his own Brahmatejas and given the child to Somada, daughter of gandharvi Urmila, who had served him faithfully and who had requested a righteous son. He later married the hundred daughters of King Kushanabha, son of King Kusha. After the departure of his hundred daughters King Kushanabha performed the 'putreshti' yagna and as a result he got a son. He was named Gadhi and in time he became the father of Vishvamitra. This ancestral detail was related by Vishvamitra to Rama and Lakshmana when they stayed overnight at Siddhashrama on their way to Mithila.

Brahmashatru

A rakshasa leader of Lanka whose house was burnt by Hanuman when he jumped from place to place with his fiery tail.

Brihaspati

Guru of devas who, by using miraculous medicinal herbs, had revived and nursed back to good health the devas who had fallen in battle against daityas in earlier times. Recalling this,

Sushena suggested that Hanuman be sent to the mountains Chandra and Drona to obtain these herbs to revive Rama and Lakshmana who had been rendered unconscious by Ravana's son Indrajit.

Budha

Son of Chandra. He fell in love with Ilaa who was King Ila of Bahlika, son of Kardama rishi. He was cursed to become alternately a female (Ilaa) for one month and male for another.

C

Chakramali

A rakshasa minister of Ravana. He was killed in battle when the forces of Rama attacked Lanka.

Chanchalakshmi

A vidyadhara woman who cursed the daitya King Sahastramukha that he would be killed by Lakshmidevi. The curse was a sequel to her being molested by the King.

Chanda

One of the many leaders of the vanara sena. In describing the strength of Rama's army, Sarana pointed him out to Ravana saying that he was a terrible warrior always looking for a fight.

Chandodari

During Seeta's enforced confinement by Ravana in Ashokavana forest, many rakshasis were guarding her. They were ordered to frighten Seeta and persuade her to yield to Ravana's advances. Among these rakshasis was the cruel Chandodari who threatened to eat Seeta's flesh.

Chandraketu

One of two sons of Lakshmana and Urmila. He was made the chief of the newly established city of Chandrakanta. (See Angada)

Chitraratha

A senior palace employee to whom Rama gave away many gifts before going into his fourteen year exile.

Chulee

A rishi who was attended upon by Somada, a daughter of gandharvee Urmila. Somada served Chulee rishi faithfully for a long time and then requested him to give her a righteous son with brilliance just like his own. Thus was born Chulee rishi's 'manasaputra' Brahmadatta.

D

Dadhimukha

An old vanara who was the maternal uncle of Sugreeva. He was assigned the duty of guarding the Madhuvana forest which was the ancestral property of Sugreeva. Hanuman after meeting Seeta in Ashokavana, was on his way back, along with other vanaras, to convey the good news to Rama. The party stopped at Madhuvana and partook of its delicious and intoxicating fruits. Dadhimukha tried to stop them but he was out-numbered and overpowered. He then went to Sugreeva to report the destruction of Madhuvana. Instead of getting angry, Sugreeva was overjoyed as he guessed that the vanaras who had been sent in the southern direction must have located Seeta; He felt that the vanaras were in a celebratory mood or else they would not have even entered Madhuvana without permission. He then reported this to Rama who asked Dadhimukha to return to Madhuvana and ask the vanaras to give an account of their search.

Danda

Youngest of the one hundred sons of Ikshvaku. He was assigned the city of Madhumana in the

Vindhya mountain range where he lived peacefully with Shukracharya as his royal priest. Once, while out in the forest, he happened to pass by Shukracharya's ashrama where he saw the guru's very pretty daughter Arja. Driven by lust the King molested Arja. When Shukracharya saw his weeping daughter and learnt all about the King's misbehaviour, he pronounced a severe curse - a blinding duststorm would destroy everything and everyone in his kingdom during the next seven days. Accompanied by his disciples, the guru left the King's realm to a safer place. A thick layer of sand soon covered the entire kingdom and all forms of life perished there. The forest came to be known as Dandakaranya. This history of early times was related by Agastya rishi to Rama while he had stopped at the rishi's hermitage on his way back from Lanka to Ayodhya.

Danu

Father of rakshasa Kabandha who advised Rama to enter into friendship with Sugreeva in order to locate Seeta.

Darimukha

A vanara commander who, along with his forces, presented himself before Sugreeva so that they could collectively undertake the task of locating Seeta who had been kidnapped by Ravana.

Dashagreeva

Name given to Ravana at birth because he had ten heads.

Dasharatha

Illustrious King of Ayodhya and descendent of the Ikshvaku dynasty. He had three wives. With Kaushalya he had Rama, of Sumitra he had Lakshmana and Shatrughna and of Kaikeyi he had Bharata. The following two events shaped his life.

In his youth, he accidentally killed with an arrow Shravana, a young man who, in the darkness of night, was collecting water for his blind and invalid father. Unable to live without Shravana, who was his only support, the father gave up his own life in utter sorrow and misery. But before dying he cursed that one day Dasharatha would also die while pining away and waiting for the return of his son.

The second incident occurred when he was grievously wounded while fighting in a battle against the asura leader Timidhwaja (also known as Shambarasura), Queen Kaikeyi then took up the reins of the fallen charioteer and saved the life of the King who then offered to fulfil two of her desires. Kaikeyi did not ask for anything at that time but said that she would do so in future at an appropriate time.

On the eve of Rama's coronation as the Crown Prince, at the instigation of her maid Manthra, she reminded the King of his earlier promise to grant two of her wishes. She then asked that Rama be exiled to the forest for fourteen years and that her own son Bharata be installed as the Crown Prince instead. Dasharatha tried his best to dissuade Kaikeyi from exacting such a cruel price for his earlier promise saying that Rama had done no wrong and that it would be impossible for him to live without his beloved son. But Kaikeyi was adamant and Dasharatha was duty-bound to keep his word. Thus it was that Rama went into forest exile to enable his father to honour his plighted word. But King Dasharatha could not bear the injustice done to his beloved son and died a heart-broken man pining for Rama. Thus was fulfilled the curse of Shravana's father. (See Shravana)

Devantaka

A rakshasa commander of Ravana's forces. He fought valiantly for his master but was no match for the all powerful Hanuman who killed him in a hand-to-hand fight in the Lankan war.

Devarata

Son of King Nimi and an early ancestor of King Janaka of Mithila. The Devas had given him a mighty bow for safe-keeping. He threatened to kill all the Devas for attending the yagna of Daksha prajapati. Shiva was not invited for the yagna and Sati, Daksha's daughter and Shiva's spouse immolated herself in protest. This bow became a family heirloom and eventually came to King Janaka. No one could even lift it, let alone string it. Rama performed this seemingly impossible task and thereby obtained the hand of Seeta.

Devavarnini

Beautiful daughter of mahamuni Bharadwaja, wife of muni Vishrawa, and mother of Vaishravana, who became Kubera with the blessings of Brahma.

Devavati

Daughter of gandharva Gramani. She married rakshasa Sukesha and had three sons: Malyavan, Sumali and Mali.

Dhanyamalini

One of the several rakshasis in Ashokavatika tasked to frighten Seeta and force her to yield to Ravana. She tried to argue with Ravana that he should not covet any female who did not reciprocate his love and desire. She had a son, Atikaya.

Dharmabhruta

A rishi, who while travelling through Dandakaranya forest, related to Rama the history of the Panchasara lake which had been created by Mandakarni rishi.

Dharmapala

One of the ministers/counsellors of King Dasharatha.

Dhrushti

One of the eight counsellors of King Dasharatha.

Dhumra

Elder brother of Jambavan, the leader of the bears. Along with his forces he presented himself before Rama to help him in his fight against Ravana.

Dhumraksha

One of the commanders of Ravana's rakshasa forces who fought against Rama's army of vanaras but was ultimately killed by Hanuman.

Dileepa

Great grandson of King Sagara, son of Anshuman. Sixty thousand sons of Sagara had perished in their search for the sacrificial horse let out by Sagara. These sons found the horse at the Kapilashrama. They attacked Kapila (an incarnate of Lord Vashudeva mistaking him as the one who stole the horse. Kapila reduced them to a heap of ashes by his snort. Dileepa wanted to bring Ganga to the earth so that when the river flowed over the ashes, the dead would attain salvation. Dileepa could not do anything. Where he failed, his son Bhageeratha succeded. (See Bhageeratha)

Diti

Mother of daityas–wife of Kashyapa rishi and sister of Aditi, mother of the devas.

Dradhanetra

One of the four sons of Vishvamitra–brother of Harishpanda, Madhushpanda and Maharatha.

Dundubhi

Son of Maya danava and younger brother of Mayavi. He assumed the form of an immense wild buffalo and harassed innocent rishis. Once he challenged the Himalaya mountain for a fight but the mountain suggested that Vali, the King of Kishkindha, would be a more worthy opponent. So he dared Vali and, after a grim prolonged battle, was killed by Vali and thrown far away.

Later, when Sugreeva doubted if Rama had enough strength to overpower Vali, Rama threw Dundubhi's body to a much greater distance by merely using the force of his big toe. This convinced Sugreeva that Rama was indeed capable of killing Vali and restoring the throne of Kishkindha, to himself.

Durdhara

One of Ravana's ministers.

Durdharsha

One of the commanders of Ravana's army who was sent out to capture Hanuman who had played havoc in Lanka. But he proved to be of no match to Hanuman who killed him by throwing his immense body on the rakshasa commander's chariot.

Durimukha

A vanara leader who along with his forces, presented himself before Sugreeva and offered help in the search for Seeta.

Durjaya

One of the leaders of the army of Khara who mounted an attack on Rama and Lakshmana in the Dandakaranya forest to avenge the disfigurement of his sister Surpanakha. In the battle that ensued Durjaya was killed along with many other rakshasas.

Durmukha

A rakshasa who, in the assembly called by Ravana, boasted that he was capable enough to teach Hanuman and Rama's army of apes a lesson.

Durmukhi

One of the several rakshasis who tried in vain to frighten Seeta and persuade her to give in to Ravana's amorous advances.

Durvasa

A rishi who, towards the end of Rama's life on

the earth, came to Ayodhya and insisted upon seeing Rama immediately. But he was stopped at the gate by Lakshmana who had been instructed by Rama not to let anyone in while a messenger of kala (fate, destiny) was delivering an important confidential message from Brahma, the Creator, on condition that any person who saw them during the delivery of the message would have to be killed by Rama. Lakshmana was fully aware of this condition and was therefore naturally reluctant to interrupt them to announce the arrival of Durvasa rishi. Durvasa then became adamant, threatening to curse not only Lakshmana but the whole Raghu dynasty and even the entire city of Ayodhya. Lakshmana then had no choice but to enter the room where kala's messenger was engaged in confidential conversation with Rama. Durvasa was ushered in and the rishi told Rama that after a prolonged period of penance, he was hungry and wanted food. After partaking of a hearty meal he disappeared from there. But Rama was duty-bound to keep his word to kill Lakshmana who had interrupted his secret meeting with kala's messenger. Seeing Rama's hesitation, Lakshmana insisted on Rama keeping his word and killing him. With great reluctance Rama then disowned his beloved brother which was equivalent to killing him. This led to Lakshmana ending his earthly existence.

Dushana

During the bloody battle in Lanka, Khara, a

cousin of Ravana, was in mortal danger. A commander, Dushana, tried to help him by attacking Rama. He fought bravely but Rama cut off his hands and killed him.

Dvivida

A great vanara–brother of Mainda. The brothers were created by the Ashwani kumaras to help Rama. Along with their forces they presented themselves before Sugreeva who was assembling an army to help Rama to look for Seeta who had been abducted. These brothers had received a boon that no one would be able to kill them in battle. They were much helpful in the war.

E

Ekajata

A rakshasi who tried in vain to persuade Seeta to accept Ravana as her husband.

G

Gadhi

King of Kaanyakubja. Son of Kushambu or Kushanabha. Gadhi was married to Ghosha. They had a daughter named Satyavati who was given in marriage to Richika rishi with whose blessings she had a son, Jamadagni, the father of Parshurama. Ghosha later became the mother of Vishvamitra.

Gaja

A vanara leader who joined Sugreeva in the search for Seeta.

Gandhamadana

When Vishnu took avatar on the earth as King Dasharatha's son Rama, Brahma asked the devas to produce valiant sons in vanara form to assist Rama. Thus it was that Gandhamadana was produced through the grace of Kubera. During the attack on Lanka under the leadership of Sugreeva, he took charge of the left flank of the army.

Ganga

Daughter of Himavan. Famous as the holiest of all rivers.

Gargya

Brahmarishi Gargya was the son of Angira rishi and royal priest of King Yudhajita of Kekaya. Towards the end of Rama's sojourn on the earth King Yudhajita sent him to Rama with a suggestion that the gandharva Kingdom of King Sailusha along the banks of the Sindhu river be conquered and joined with the Kingdom of Ayodhya. This task was accomplished by Bharata and later his sons, Taksha and Pushkala, were put in charge of the newly conquered territories.

Gautama

A rishi who had cursed his wife Ahalya for engaging in an illicit affair with Indra. In accordance with this curse, Ahalya remained in a petrified lifeless form in front of their ashrama. When Rama, on his way to Mithila, passed by this ashrama and encountered the formless Ahalya, she got back her lovely human form and was reunited with Gautama rishi after the brothers had touched her feet. She had remained invisible till she saw Rama.

Gavaksha

Produced in his own image by Yama, this vanara leader was a fearless combatant in Sugreeva's army.

Gavaya

Yama had produced him from his own element

as a vanara leader known for his boast that he could destroy single-handedly Ravana's rakshasa forces.

Golabha

A gandharva who was killed by Vali after a prolonged battle.

Gomukha

Son of Indra's charioteer Matali. During a fierce battle between devas and rakshasas he drove the chariot of Indra's son, Jayanta, who fought with Ravana's son, Meghanada.

Guha

King of Bhila community in the region of Sringiberapara. He received Rama, Lakshmana and Seeta on their way to Dandakaranya. He welcomed them with open arms and then provided them with a boat to go across the Ganga.

When Bharata, along with Shatrughna, the three Queens of King Dasharatha and the royal entourage, came there in search of Rama, Guha at first suspected their intention. But upon meeting Bharata and learning that he had come there only to persuade Rama to return to Ayodhya, he welcomed them and helped the royal party to cross the Ganga.

H

Hanuman

Physically strong, intellectually eminent, Hanuman is the linchpin of the vanara sena. A vanara minister of Sugreeva, Hanuman was a great devotee of Rama (Rama-bhakta) whom he served valiantly and successfully, yet with great modesty. He was born of Kesari and Anjana, of the vanara tribe. He is also described as the son of the Wind-god Vayu.

In his childhood, when he mistook the rising sun for a fruit, he jumped up in the sky to catch it. On his way, jealous of his power and speed, Indra hurled his thunder bolt at him and he fell on the mountain-side. He broke his jaw, (Hanu) and hence earned his name 'Hanuman'. Vayu then entered into a combat with Indra but Brahma intervened and stopped their fight. After that all the devas blessed Hanuman and Brahma gave him various weapons and boons by which he became invincible. A little later, however, rishis Angira and Bhrugu pronounced a curse saying that he would not be aware of his extraordinary strength but that only a divine person would be able to recognize his valour and use it to his advantage.

He befriended Sugreeva, the exiled King of Kishkindha and later he became his counsellor and trusted aide. It was he who first spotted Rama and Lakshmana in Dandakaranya as they were searching for the kidnapped Seeta. He was instrumental in cementing the lifelong friendship between Rama and Sugreeva to the benefit of both.

When Sugreeva assembled the vanara forces to assist Rama in locating Seeta, Hanuman was assigned as the leader of the team going in the southern direction with instructions to report back within 30 days. On the way, he encountered Sampati, elder brother of Jatayu,who described how Ravana had abducted Seeta and that she was in captivity in Ashokavana in Lanka. After all the vanaras, one by one, had expressed their inability to jump across the ocean to reach Lanka, old Jambavan recalled Hanuman's origin and reminded him of his own strength and capability. Hanuman then felt inspired and was filled with determination to succeed in the task assigned by Rama. He then assumed a gigantic size and leapt from mount Mahendra all the way to Lanka. On his way mount Mainaka, which was submerged under the ocean, rose above ground to provide a resting spot for him. But not wanting to waste any time, he did not avail of this kind offer.

Surasa, the mother of nagas, and Simhika, a rakshasi, tried to thwart him in attaining his objective. But Hanuman overcame them and finally landed on mount Trikuta in Lanka. Upon landing there he once again reduced himself to his normal size.

Knowing that it was almost impossible for any unauthorized person to enter Ravana's fortress city, he waited until dusk and then, reducing himself to the size of a cat tried to go inside the fort. But he was spotted and stopped by Lanka's deity, Lankaa. Hanuman tried to cajole her but finally had to knock her down before going inside the city. After a while he located Ashokavana and there finally he saw Seeta sitting under a tree, distraught. He identified himself by showing her a ring given to him by Rama and he assured her that Rama was on his way to free her. He even offered to carry her back to Rama but she refused saying that she was entitled to be saved by Rama only. Before departing from Ashokavana, he uprooted many magnificent old trees and destroyed the beautiful gardens.

Upon learning of this destruction Ravana became furious and sent a force to capture Hanuman but they were easily overpowered. Finally, Ravana's son Indrajit used the "Brahmastra" weapon and brought Hanuman bound before the rakshasa court. Now Hanuman knew that because of an earlier curse, he would have to suffer temporarily from the "Brahmastra". So he allowed himself to be captured and paraded around the town so that he may assess the position and strength of the enemy forces. As Hanuman was an emissary of Rama, his life was spared but Ravana ordered that his tail be set on fire before he was let loose. Through the grace of god Agni, Hanuman did not feel the heat even when his tail was burning. Instead, he flew all over the city's tall buildings setting them on fire with his burning tail. After creating this terrible havoc in Lanka he returned to Sugreeva and related all his exploits to Rama. In order to provide a convincing proof that he had actually met Seeta, he presented to Rama a crest-jewel (choodamani) which Seeta had given him for this purpose and he also repeated an episode from an earlier time related to him by Seeta and which was not known to anyone else.

Hanuman played a prominent role in the Lankan war. He killed Akampana, a formidable foe. He lifted up a distant mountain peak that contained shining herbs and brought it to the battlefield wherein Rama and Lakshmana, along with 67 crore apes, lay unconscious, bound as they were by Brahmastra aimed at them by Indrajit. When the unconscious royal brothers and the vanaras caught the scent of the medicinal herbs they woke up as if from a long sleep. Hanuman once again brought the herbs-bearing mountain, when Lakshmana was grievously wounded by Ravana.

At his coronation Rama gave Hanuman beautiful ornaments and a pair of splendid spotted clothes. While doing so, he was looking at Seeta. Janaki, in turn, unlocking a necklace of pearls from her neck, looked at Rama. The king, reading her mind, told her "Give the necklace, O fortunate one, to whom and with whom you are vastly pleased because in whom are combined power and courage, fame and capability, skill and shrewdness, manliness, valour and intellectuality." The queen did so, to Hanuman who shone bright like a white cloud in a mountain peak bathed in moonlight.

It is believed (as a verse says) that wherever Rama's story is told even to-day, Hanuman, hidden from view, listens to it with his eyes filled with tears, head bowed in reverence.

Hanuman is considered as one of the immortals.

Hara

A great vanara chief with a long yellow tail which shone like gold in sunlight.

Hara

Rakshasa son of Mali and Ravana's uncle.

Harijata

When Seeta was kept captive in Ashokavana, this cat-eyed rakshasi tried to induce her to marry

Ravana whom she described as the victor of the devas including Indra.

Hasavaroma

Father of King Janaka of Mithila and grandfather of Seeta. His other son was Kushadhwaja.

Havishpanda

One of the four sons of rishi Vishvamitra.

Hayagreeva

An asura resident of mount Chakravana. After slaying him and his brother Panchayana, Vishnu had obtained the divine thousand-pointed chakra and the Panchajanya shankha.

Hema

Mother-in-law of Ravana. One of the favourite apsarases of Indra. She married Maya danava and lived for a long time in the forest created by her husband. After giving birth to a daughter, Mandodari, she returned to swarga.

Hemakuta

Born from an element of Varuna; he was one of the chiefs in the army of vanaras led by Sugreeva.

Hemamali

A rakshasa commander who had accompanied Khara during their abortive attack on Rama at Panchavati. Along with other rakshasas he was killed by Rama.

Heti

Along with his brother, Praheti, he was created by Brahma at the beginning of time in order to protect the seas. He married Yama's sister, Bhaya, who then gave birth to Vidyutakesha, an early ancestor of Ravana's mother Kaikasi.

Himalaya

Called the King of mountains he married Mena, the daughter of mount Meru. They had two daughters: Ganga the holy river and Uma or Parvati who married Shiva.

Hutashuna

Father of the vanaras, Ulkamukha and Ananga, who took part in the expedition to the south sent by Sugreeva in search of Seeta.

I

Idmavaha

Younger brother of the great Agastya rishi. Rama, Lakshmana and Seeta, on their way to Agastya's ashrama, stayed overnight at Idmavaha rishi's ashrama.

Ikshvaku

Founder of the illustrious royal lineage of Ayodhya. Son of apsara Alambusha. His son Vishala, founded the city of Vishalanagari which was being ruled by King Sumati when Vishvamitra, along with Rama and Lakshmana, passed through the city on their way to Mithila.

Ila and Ilaa

King Ila was the son of Prajapati Kardama and he ruled righteously over the land of Bahlika. Once while out on a hunt, he entered that part of the forest where Kartikeya (Subrahamanya–Muruga or Skanda) was born. There Mahadeva having taken the form of a female, was amusing himself with Parvati. As soon as king Ila came to that private area of the forest he was turned into a woman and in that state she surrendered to Mahadeva who agreed to give him any boon other than regaining his manhood. Ila was disappointed and did not ask for any boon but devi Parvati agreed to give him half a boon. There upon Ila asked that he remain a male for one month and a woman for next month alternatively. After granting this boon both Mahadeva and Parvati disappeared from the scene.

King Ila in his female form became Ilaa, a beautiful maiden. Wandering in the forest Ilaa once encountered Chandra's (Soma's) son Budha who fell in love with her and they began to live together happily. When the month was over King Ila woke up from bed as though from a deep sleep and expressed his desire to return to Bahlika. But Budha prevailed upon him to stay there for a year. When in male form Ila held religious and philosophical discussions with Budha while in female form as Ilaa she enjoyed conjugal life with Budha. Thus it was that Ilaa gave birth to a son, Pururavas.

Budha then assembled all the learned rishis and conducted an ashwamedha yagna. This pleased Mahadeva immensely and he made King Ila permanently a male.

Rama related this episode of early history to Lakshmana and Bharata to underline the importance of ashwamedha yagna and then decided to hold such a one himself.

Ilvala

A rakshasa who used to get his brother Vatapi to assume the form of a goat which he killed, cooked and served to the invited rishis. He then called out his dead brother and through the art of Sanjivani, Vatapi emerged by tearing through the stomachs of the unsuspecting guests. In this way he killed many rishis.

Indrajanu

A vanara leader who, along with his forces, joined the army of Sugreeva to help Rama locate Seeta and then fight against the rakshasa army of Ravana.

Indrajit (Meghanada)

Beloved son of Ravana and Mandodari. Immediately after he was born, the child Indrajit cried like rain and thunder and was therefore named Meghanada. He became well known as Indrajit after his victory over Indra.

Under the guidance of guru Shukracharya he performed innumerable yagnas but later discontinued this practice when he realized that the devas who were sworn enemies of his father, were getting a share of the benefits accruing from such yagnas. When Ravana went to swarga to fight against the devas, he accompanied his father and, capturing Indra, he brought him in a captive state to Lanka. All the devas, under the leadership of

Brahma, then went to Lanka to secure Indra's release. Brahma blessed Indrajit and offered to grant him any boon other than that of immortality. Thereupon Indrajit requested that whenever he performed a yagna at Nikumbhilaa, a divine chariot with horses should emerge and that as long as he fought from that chariot, he would be invincible and no one would be able to kill him. Upon receiving this boon Indra was released.

In the ultimate battle against the forces of Rama, Indrajit fought valiantly using his powers of illusion. On one occasion he felled both Rama and Lakshmana and tied them up with poisonous snakes but Garuda saved them later by driving away the snakes. Later, using the ultimate weapon Brahmastra he knocked down Rama and Lakshmana unconscious. Again they were saved when Hanuman brought the divine sanjivanee herbal medicines from the Himalayas. Finally, he sat down at Nikumbhila to perform the yagna which would give him the divine chariot from which he would be invincible. But Vibhishana who knew this secret asked the vanara forces to attack him there and ensure that the yagna was not completed. This the vanaras achieved. In the final prolonged battle with Lakshmana, which went on for three days and three nights, he lost his life.

Ishmavaha

Brother of Agastya rishi.

J

Jabali

A rishi who, along with Kashyapa, Gautama, Markendya and others, served as counsellor to King Dasharatha of Ayodhya.

Jahnu

A great muni who had once swallowed the river Ganga which had drowned his ashrama while following King Anshuman. Later at the request of all rishis, he released the great Ganga which from then on was known as his daughter Jahnavi.

Jamadagni

A renowned rishi. Son of Satyavati, sister of sage Vishvamitra. It was his slaying by the Haihaya King Sahasrarjuna which led to his son Parshurama to kill all kshatriyas.

Jambasura

His son Sunda married Tataka, the daughter of yaksha Suketu.

Jambavan

King of bears. He united his forces with the

vanara army of Sugreeva to aid Rama in locating and freeing Seeta.

Jambavan

An old vanara chief who reminded Hanuman about the divine nature of his birth and then inspired him to undertake the difficult task of leaping over the ocean to reach Lanka in the search for Seeta.

Jambavan

Son of vanara Gadragada and brother of Kesari. He fought valiantly in support of Rama in the battle for Lanka. At the coronation of Rama he brought holy water for the ceremonies. For Rama's ashwamedha yagna he went along with Shatrughna to protect the horse.

Janaka

Father of Seeta and father-in-law of Rama. His ancestor was Mithi after whom his city was named. He had inherited from his ancestor Devarata, the mighty bow used by Shankara to destroy the yagna conducted by Prajapati Daksha. While ploughing a sacrificial site to cleanse it, he found a girl child in the furrow. It was Seeta. The King and Queen brought her up as their daughter. The King decided that he would give Seeta in marriage only to the one who showed his valour by lifting Shiva's bow and stringing it.

Jatayu

Depicted as the King of vultures, he was a

descendent of Kashyapa Prajapati and his fifth wife Tamra. He and his elder brother Sampati were born of Aruna and Shyeni. When he first encountered Rama, Lakshmana and Seeta while they were on their way to set up their ashrama at Panchavati, he was already very old and had lost much of his strength. Yet, as a friend of King Dasharatha, he stayed on with them at Panchavati to offer protection to Seeta while the two brothers were away.

When he heard the piteous wail of Seeta being carried away by Ravana, he flew up and fought valiantly to free Seeta. But he was no match for Ravana who, after a bloody struggle, cut off his wings and the old bird fell to the ground in a helpless state. When Rama and Lakshmana found him drawing his last breath, all he could say was that Ravana had carried away Seeta and flown in a southern direction . With tender care Rama cremated his body.

Java

A rakshasa–husband of Shatahrada and father of rakshasa Viradha who had confronted Rama, Lakshmana and Seeta when they had entered Dandakaranya at the beginning of their exile.

Jaya

Wife of Prajapati Kashyapa.

Jayanta

After the death of Dasharatha, Jayanta was

one of the messengers sent to Rajagraha to fetch Bharata and Shatrughna to Ayodhya. He was one of the eight ministers of Dasharatha.

Jayanta

Son of Indra. At the instance of his father he once assumed the form of a crow and bit and bled Seeta while Rama was resting with his head on her lap. Though suffering much pain Seeta did not disturb the sleeping Rama. Waking up, Rama felt that Seeta had suffered in silence. He then picked up a blade of grass and, intoning a divine mantra, threw it at the crow which then fled from there. Even after the crow had roamed over the three worlds with the blade of grass following it, no one offered to protect it. Finally, it surrendered to Rama who pardoned it after blinding it in the right eye.

This episode which had occurred on the banks of river Mandakini was known only to Rama and Seeta. When Hanuman had located Seeta in Ashokavana and was preparing for his return journey, Seeta narrated this episode with the instruction that he should relate it to Rama in order to assure him that Hanuman had indeed seen her.

Jyotirmukha

Born as a vanara from an element of Surya, he was one of the commanders of Sugreeva's army in aid of Rama.

K

Kabandha

Born as gandharva Vishwavasu, he had a very strong body. He used to assume the form of a ferocious rakshasa and harass innocent rishis in the forest. Once when he offended rishi Sthulashira, the latter cursed that Kabandha would remain in rakshasa form for the rest of his life and that he would regain his original form when Rama cut off his arms and cremated the body.

In his rakshasa form Kabandha undertook prolonged penances and acquired from Brahma a boon for a long life. With this boon he once again became arrogant and attacked Indra who overpowered him. In order to respect Brahma's boon Indra did not kill the rakshasa but merely cut off his legs and pushed his head into his torso. Kabandha then pleaded to be put to death as, without his ability to move around and consume food he would die anyway. Indra then caused the rakshasa's arms to be elongated so that he may catch his prey from a distance. He also caused the rakshasa to have an artificial mouth in his torso. It was in this hideous form that the rakshasa became known as Kabandha. He then continued to live in the forest waiting to be delivered by Rama.

When Rama and Lakshmana began their search for Seeta they were caught by Kabandha in his long arms. But, just as he was about to devour them, Rama cut off his arms and Kabandha realized that his salvation was near. He then promised to help Rama after regaining his original form. When Rama cremated the rakshasa's body there arose from the flames the original human form which suggested that Rama should make the exiled Sugreeva as his chief ally. After giving Rama explicit directions about reaching Kishkindha, he gave up his life and rose to swarga.

Kaikasi

Mother of Ravana, Kumbhakarna, Surpanakha and Vibhishana. Wife of Vaishrava muni and daughter of Sumali rakshasa. At the wrong time of the day she pressed her husband to have coitus. The muni cursed that her children would be born as wicked rakshasas. When she repented for her folly, he said that her youngest child would be righteous and follow dharma. That was Vibhishana.

Kaikeyi

Kaikeyi was the youngest, prettiest and the most favoured of King Dasharatha's three Queens. She was the daughter of King Ashwapati of Kekaya. Her brother was called Yudhajita. Her son was Bharata.

Soon after her wedding, King Dasharatha fought against the daityas in defence of the devas. He was grievously wounded and his chariot was badly damaged. Queen Kaikeyi, disregarding her own safety, managed to take the King out of the battlefield and thus saved his life. King Dasharatha was very much pleased and offered to fulfill two of her wishes, if any. She said that she would tell him at an appropriate time.

On the eve of Rama's coronation as the Crown Prince, Kaikeyi was in a happy frame of mind. She was as fond of Rama as she was of her own son Bharata. But Kaikeyi's wicked maid, Manthara, who had been with her from childhood, poisoned her mind by saying that once Rama ascended the throne, she and her own son Bharata would be neglected. Further, she reminded the Queen about her husband's offer of granting her wishes. She then went on to suggest that she should ask that Rama be exiled to the forest for fourteen years and that Bharata be crowned as the King in his place. Thinking that Manthara's advice was in her interest, Kaikeyi put these two requests before King Dasharatha who had no alternative but to agree. Soon after Rama's departure the grief-stricken Dasharatha died.

Contrary to expectations, Bharata refused to be crowned as the King and insisted that Rama be recalled from the forest and crowned. He called his own mother greedy, proud and devoid of righteousness. Kaikeyi is looked upon as an evil-minded character of the epic.

Kakutstha

A King of the Ishwaku dynasty. Father of Vishala who had founded the city of Vishalanagari. When passing through their city, rishi Vishvamitra narrated to Rama the lineage of this King. In the battle between devas and daityas he had agreed to fight on behalf of the devas only if he could do so sitting on the back (Kakut) of Indra. After his success, he came to be called Kakutstha–one who sat on the back.

Kalaa

Daughter of Vibhishana. She was sympathetic to Seeta and had once told her how her father failed in persuading Ravana to return her to Rama.

Kalindi

Kalindi was one of the two wives of King Asita. The King was driven out of his Kingdom by his enemies, and he died in a forest. Kalindi then was expecting a child. Out of envy and jealousy the other wife poisoned her but because of the grace of Chyavana rishi, whom Kalindi had served faithfully, she did not die. She gave birth to a healthy baby boy who was immune to poison. He was named Sagara endowed with strength, valour and power. He regained his father's kingdom and became an illustrious ruler. Among his descendants were King Dasharatha and Rama.

This episode was narrated by Vasishtha while telling Janaka about the lineage of King Dasharatha.

Kalkarmuka

One of the twelve rakshasa leaders who accompanied Khara in his battle against Rama at Panchavati to avenge the ill-treatment of his sister Surpanakha. After a fierce battle he, along with other rakshasas, was killed by Rama.

Kamadhenu (Shabala)

Divine cow of Vasishta rishi. It fulfilled all human desires. It was forcefully taken away from him by Vishvamitra (as King).

Kampana

After the death of Kumbhakarna, the rakshasa forces were regrouping inside the walled city. Sugreeva then ordered that the vanara army should set fire to all houses surrounding the fortress. The rakshasas were then forced to come out in battle formation against the vanara army. Among the rakshasa forces was Kampana who was a great fighter. However, he proved to be of no match to the mighty Angada who killed him in a fierce fight.

Kanchana

Towards the end of Rama's mortal life, Shatrughna was put in charge of the Kingdom of Mathura. At that time Kanchana was his minister.

Kandu

A rishi of early times who, in order to abide by his father's word, had committed the heinous crime of killing a cow. This was cited by Rama to his mother Kaushalya to explain to her why it was of paramount importance for him to enable his father King Dasharatha to keep his word.

Kandu

A great rishi whose son had been taken away by death when he was only ten years old. In despair and anger he then cursed that the forest in which this happened be rendered unfit for habitation by humans, animals, birds, etc. Angada, Hanuman and other vanaras, in search for Seeta, went through this forest.

Kartikeya (Skanda)

Born from Shiva's seed of life, swallowed by Agni and deposited in Ganga at the foothills of the Himalayas, he was nourished by six krittikas and hence named Kartikeya. Elder brother of Ganesha, he was a valiant fighter as the commander-in-chief of the devas.

Karviraksha

When Khara rakshasa mounted an attack against Rama to take revenge for the ill-treatment of his sister Surpanakha, Karviraksha was one of the leaders of Khara's army. He, along with Khara and many other rakshasa leaders, was killed by Rama at Panchavati.

Kashyapa

Husband of Diti and Aditi who became the mothers of danavas and devas respectively. At the conclusion of prolonged penances, when Vishnu appeared before him and offered to grant him a boon, Kashyapa requested that Vishnu himself be born in his house. Thus it was that Vishnu took avatara as Vamana the dwarf and subdued the danava King Bali by putting his foot on his head and pressing him down into the subterranean world. This episode of early history was narrated by rishi Vishvamitra to Rama while they were passing by Siddhashrama, the place of Kashyapa's penance.

Katyayana

One of the several learned rishis serving as counsellors to King Dasharatha.

Kaushalya

Mother of Rama. Eldest of King Dasharatha's three Queens—daughter of King Bhanumana of

Koshala. Gentle by nature and righteous in behaviour, she was extremely fond of Rama. Yet, she agreed reluctantly to Rama's exile because she felt that it was Rama's duty to enable his father to keep the word given to Queen Kaikeyi. Along with Bharata and the rest of the royal household she went into the forest to persuade Rama to return to Ayodhya. After the completion of Rama's forest exile and his return to Ayodhya, she spent many peaceful years as Queen Mother during Rama's reign.

Kekaya

Father of Kaikeyi. He had received a boon by which he could understand the language of animals and birds but he was destined to die if he told anyone of what they spoke. Once when the King and the Queen were together, King Kekaya heard a bird say something to its mate. Having understood the bird's language the King started laughing. The Queen asked the King, why he was laughing, suspecting that he was laughing at her. But he declined to give the reason as the disclosure of it would mean his death. Even after knowing this, the Queen insisted on getting an explanation, adding that it would not matter if he lived or not. Because of this senseless insistence the King abandoned her.

This episode was recalled by counsellor Sumantra to tell Kaikeyi that she had inherited her obstinate trait from her mother.

Kesari

Father of Hanuman, husband of Anjana. He, along with the vanara forces of Sumeru, joined Sugreeva to help locate Seeta and then fight against the rakshasas in Lanka.

Keshini

Elder of the two Queens of King Sagara. She was the daughter of the King of Vidarbha. After prolonged attendance on Bhrugu rishi the King obtained a boon that one of his Queens would give birth to a son who would continue the royal lineage while the other Queen would give birth to sixty thousand sons who would be valiant fighters. Keshini preferred to give birth to one son and that was Asamanjasa whose great grandson Bhagiratha managed to persuade Ganga to come down to the earth.

Ketumali

Wife of rakshasa Sumali, mother of Kaikasi and grandmother of Ravana. She was the daughter of gandharvi Narmada.

Khara

Rakshasa cousin of Ravana. His mother, Pushpotaka, and Ravana's mother, Kaikasi, were sisters. When Surpanakha was disfigured and humiliated, she went crying to her brother Khara and urged him to kill Seeta whom she regarded as the source of all her troubles. Khara sent fourteen rakshasas to do this job but they were killed by Rama. Khara then led a force of fourteen thousand rakshasas but they did not fare any better. Only Trishira and he escaped with their lives. Livid with rage, Khara mobilised a larger force and attacked Rama once again. Even then Rama got the better of the entire rakshasa force and, after a prolonged and fierce battle, killed both Trishira and Khara.

Krathanathe

A vanara leader, who, under the leadership of Sugreeva, fought valiantly against Ravana's rakshasa forces. He was born of Agni and a gandharva maiden and in earlier times he had fought on the side of the devas against asuras. He resided on mount Kailasagiri, the abode of Kubera.

Krushasva

A prajapati who had produced some divine weapons. But since he had given up arms, he regarded these as his sons. While Vishvamitra was still a King before he became a rishi, he had undertaken penances and earned the pleasure of Mahadeva who gave him these weapons as his sons.

Kubera (Vaishravana)

Lord of Wealth. Along with Indra, Varuna and

Yama he was the fourth lokapala and leader of the yakshas. Son of Paulastya (better known as Vishravas and Devavarnini (also known as Idwila) daughter of rishi Bhardawaja, he was the grandson of prajapati Pulastya. He was half-brother of Ravana whose mother Kaikasi was the second wife of Vishravas.

He had pleased Brahma through prolonged penances and obtained from him the designation of lokapala in charge of wealth. Brahma also gave him a divine vimana known as Pushpaka which could take him anywhere he pleased. He was assigned to rule over the island of Lanka which had been earlier abandoned by rakshasas.

Later, Ravana sent him a threatening message asking him to give back Lanka which had been ruled by his maternal grandfather Sumali. Kubera, realizing the strength of Ravana's army, left Lanka and established the city of Amaravati where he then lived happily with his wife Bhadra and sons, Manigriva and Nalakubera.

Much later, Ravana, along with Kumbhakarna and other rakshasas, attacked Amaravati. After defeating Kubera, he took away the divine Pushpaka vimana. Rama used the vehicle to fly back to Ayodhya.

Kubja

Another name of Manthara.

Kumbha

Son of Kumbhakarna and elder brother of Nikumbha. His house was one among the several that were set on fire by Hanuman with his burning tail. A very ferocious fighter in Ravana's army, he was killed by Sugreeva.

Kumbhavanu

A rakshasa leader of commander Prahasta's army. In the battle against Sugreeva's forces he was killed by Tara vanara.

Kumbhakarna

Ravana's younger brother–son of Kaikasi and Vishrava rishi–depicted as the sleeping giant of immense size. Along with Ravana and Vibhishana he undertook severe penances to please Brahma. When at last Brahma was ready to grant him a boon, the devas pleaded that he be misguided in making his request. Accordingly, Saraswati appeared on his tongue and he requested a long undisturbed sleep. This was granted by Brahma saying that he would sleep for six months and remain awake for one day.

During the early stages of the vanara attack against rakshasa forces, Kumbhakarna was fast asleep and Ravana saw no need to wake him up. But when one after another his commanders, including Prahasta, were killed, he gave orders to wake up his younger brother. A lot of food and wine was first arranged around the body of the sleeping giant and then the rakshasas began to wake him up. But that task was not easy and it took the combined efforts of thousands of rakshasas along with drum beaters and elephants to finally arouse the great giant. After consuming all that had been offered to him, he went to Ravana.

Having listened to the woes of his elder brother, Kumbhakarna first reminded him of what he had told him earlier, that it was wrong on his part to have abducted someone else's wife. But Ravana wanted him to forget the past and deal with the present danger facing them. Kumbhakarna then reluctantly agreed to enter the battlefield out of his brotherly love. With his immense size and strength he wrought havoc among the enemy forces by crushing or swallowing hundreds of vanaras at a time. On one occasion he caught hold of Sugreeva and brought him back to Lanka but, at the last moment, Sugreeva managed to escape from his grip after biting off his nose and ears. Kumbhakarna then returned to the battlefield with his bleeding face and challenged Rama to a one-to-one fight. A fierce battle then took place between gigantic strength on the one hand and divine weapons on the other. Finally, Rama cut off his arms and legs one by one and then severed his head which fell on land

and the torso fell into the ocean. Thus ended the life of the sleeping giant. He was survived by wife Vajrawala, granddaughter of Virochana daitya, and two sons, Kumbha and Nikumbha.

Kumudavati

Wife of Rama's son Kusha. She was the daughter of naga Kumuda.

Kumbhinasi

Elder sister of Ravana's mother Kaikasi, daughter of Sumali and Ketumali.

Kumbhinasi

Daughter of Ananta and Vishwavasu–granddaughter of Malyavan and Sundari. Thus, she was a second cousin of Ravana. She was abducted by Madhu daitya who then married her. They had one son by name Lavanasura.

Kumuda

A vanara chief who ruled over land in the Sarvochana mountain range. Along with his army he joined the forces of Sugreeva to locate and retrieve Seeta.

Kunjara

Vanara, maternal grandfather of Hanuman. Following a rishi's curse, apsara Punjikashali had taken birth in human form as Kunjara's daughter Anjana, who married Kesarivanara and became the mother of Hanuman.

Kusha

Elder of the twin sons of Rama and Seeta–brother of Lava. He was born in Valmiki's ashrama, where Seeta had been living after being abandoned by Rama. At the ashwamedha yagna of Rama, the twins sang Ramacharita at the suggestion of guru Valmiki. This made Rama accept them as his sons and led him recall Seeta. Before ending his earthly life Rama arranged to divide his Kingdom into two and made Kusha the King of Pushkara. Later, Kusha married Champika. He also married Kumudavati, daughter of naga Kumuda.

Kusha

A King of early times who, with Queen Vaidarbhi, had four sons: Kushamba, Kushanabha, Asurtaraja and Vasu. His history was related to Rama when he was passing by Vasumali, a city established by Vasu, along with Vishvamitra and Lakshmana.

Kushadhwaja

Younger brother of King Janaka of Mithila–father of Mandavi and Shrutakirti–father-in-law of Bharata and Shatrughna.

Kushadhwaja

Son of guru Brihaspati. He wanted his daughter Vedavati to marry Vishnu and, therefore, refused all marriage proposals from devas, gandharvas, yakshas and rakshasas. Such frequent refusals angered the daitya chief Shambhu who, in great rage, killed Kushadhwaja.

Kushamba

Eldest of the four sons of King Kusha. After the death of his father he established the city of Kushambi and ruled over it righteously.

Kushanabha

Son of King Kusha. He established the city of Mahodaya. Once he fell in love with apsara Ghrutachi, who gave birth to one hundred girls. These girls grew up to become extremely beautiful and charming young maidens. Vayu, while blowing through the skies, happened to see them and got enamoured of them. He asked all of them to marry him saying that he would ensure that they remained young and desirable for the rest of their lives. But the girls refused this offer saying that they would marry only according to the wishes of their father. Enraged at this rebuff, Vayu pronounced a curse whereby all the girls became ugly and deformed.

Weeping in misery the girls returned to the palace and related to their father all that had happened. He praised them for holding up the values of the family and not falling for the false promises which would have brought shame upon their entire family.

In due course King Kushanabha arranged the marriage of all his daughters to King Brahmadatta, son of rishi Chuli and Somada, daughter of apsara Urmila. As soon as King Brahmadatta touched the deformed girls, they returned to their original beautiful form and they lived happily.

After the departure of his daughters King Kushanabha performed a yagna for a child and his Queen gave birth to a boy who became King Gadhi, father of rishi Vishvamitra.

L

Lakshmana

Devoted younger brother of Rama, son of King Dasharatha and his second wife Sumitra and elder brother of Shatrughna and Bharata. On the occasion of Rama winning the hand of Seeta at her swayamwara, his own marriage was arranged with Urmila, daughter of King Janaka.

Lakshmana's entire life was devoted to protecting Rama and attending to his personal needs. He thus reduced his own life interests to zero and dedicated his life to the welfare of Rama. Thus he is portrayed as an ideal brother. He was short tempered and prone to angry outbursts but all in the interests of Rama. Hence these were never considered to be offensive.

Out of devotion to his brother, he voluntarily went into forest exile with Rama and Seeta. He stood guard over them at night when they were sleeping; took care of Seeta when Rama was away; collected fruits, nuts and berries for them and built their forest dwelling. He assisted Rama in overpowering demons like Viradha and he punished Ravana's sister Surpanakha.

When Rama went after the illusionary golden deer, Lakshmana was left in charge of Seeta. Upon hearing Rama's impersonated voice crying out for help, Seeta forced him to rush to Rama's aid. Lakshmana was most reluctant to leave Seeta alone but had to obey her and this led to her abduction by Ravana. He then accompanied Rama in search of Seeta. Sugreeva on one occasion showed them some gold ornaments presumably thrown down from the sky by Seeta while being carried away by Ravana. Rama wanted Lakshmana to identify the jewels.

Lakshmana identified only her anklet saying that he knew nothing about the other ornaments as he had never raised his eyes above the feet. Such was his reverence for Seeta, as Rama's spouse.

In the battle for Lanka he fought valiantly killing rakshasa stalwarts like Kumbhakarna and Indrajit. On one occasion, he was felled by Indrajit and bound along with Rama by snake bonds. However, both were saved by Garuda. On another occasion when both brothers were rendered unconscious by Indrajit, they were revived by application of herbs specially brought for this purpose by Hanuman all the way from the Himalayas.

After the coronation of Rama as the King of Ayodhya, Lakshmana was appointed as the commander-in-chief and he expanded the limits of the Kingdom. On his shoulders fell the unpleasant task of taking Seeta into the forest and abandoning her there. Even then he did not question the appropriateness of Rama's decision. Such was his faith in his brother's judgement. At the suggestion of Rama, he installed his elder son Angada as the King of Angadiapuri and younger son Chandraketu as the King of Chandrakanta.

On the last day of his life he once again performed a selfless act. A messenger of Yama, in the guise of a brahmana, came to Rama to deliver a confidential message on condition that if anyone saw them during that time, then the intruder would have to be killed. So they sat down in a closed room with Lakshmana guarding the door. Just at that time Durvasa rishi appeared there demanding to see Rama urgently. Lakshmana stopped him where upon Durvasa threatened to curse not only Rama but the entire royal family. Lakshmana was willing to give up his own life to save Rama from being cursed. So he interrupted the confidential talk and Rama was obliged to abandon him which was equivalent to killing him.

Lakshmana then gave up his life on the banks of river Saryu and his soul rose to merge with Sheshanaga from whose element he was born.

Of Lakshmana, Seeta told Hanuman that Lakshmana was dearer to Rama than herself. (Sundara Kanda)

Lankaa

Guardian deity of Ravana's Lanka. She stopped Hanuman when he wanted to get into Lanka in his search for Seeta. A fight ensued and she was felled.

She told Hanuman that her defeat would spell the destruction of the Rakshasas.

Lava

Younger of the twin sons of Seeta born in Valmiki rishi's ashrama. On the occasion of Rama's ashwamedha yagna, Lava and his elder twin Kusha sang Ramacharita which led to Rama accepting them as his sons. As the end of Rama's earthly life was approaching, he divided the Kingdom into two and put Lava in charge of southern Koshala over which he ruled righteously along with his two Queens, Sumali and Kanjana.

Lavanasura

Son of Madhu daitya and Ravana's second cousin Kumbhinasi. Lavanasura had inherited from his father a divine weapon called Shula. While gifting this weapon to Madhu daitya in recognition of his righteous behaviour towards brahmanas, Rudra deva had indicated that the Shula would kill any enemy he fought against and then return to him. With this weapon in hand Lavanasura became invincible and he began to think of himself as immortal. In his pride and arrogance he began to harass innocent rishis who finally sought the help of Rama. Shatrughna then volunteered to get rid of this tyrant and Rama instructed him to ensure that he confronted the asura only when the latter was without his divine Shula.

Shatrughna then marched to Madhupura and waited at the palace gate for the return of Lavanasura from a pleasurable outing. Not expecting any enemy he was at that time without his Shula and in the ensuing battle Shatrughna killed him. After his death the Shula returned to Rudra deva.

M

Madhuchhanda

Rishi Vishvamitra's son who refused to obey his father and exchange places with Ruchika rishi's son Sunahshepa who had been purchased by King Ambarisha to replace an animal which had to be sacrificed at his (Ambarisha's) yagna. Because of this refusal he and his brothers were cursed to lead the life of a dog-eating animal. Sunahshepa was a nephew of Vishvamitra whom the latter did not want to be sacrificed.

Madhureshwara

Even after ruling over all the three worlds, daitya King Vruta undertook penances to attain still more merits. At that time he left his son Madhureshwara in charge.

Madhushpanda

When King Vishvamitra realized the superiority of brahmana's virtues over kshatriya's strength, he decided to undertake penances to please Brahma and obtain from him the status of a great rishi. At that time four sons were born to him of whom Madhushpanda was one.

Mahakapala

A rakshasa who accompanied Khara to attack Rama in order to avenge the ill-treatment meted out to Surpanakha. In the ensuing battle he was killed by Rama. Surpanakha was a sister of Khara.

Mahamali

A rakshasa serving under Khara. He was killed by Rama.

Mahananda

Rakshasa counsellor of Prahasta who went into battle along with his chief but was killed by Jambavan.

Mahaparshwa

One of the younger brothers of Ravana. In the battle against Sugreeva's forces he was killed by vanara Rushabha.

Mahaparshwa

A rakshasa commander who was put in charge of guarding the southern gate of Lanka fort. He was killed by Angada in the war.

Maharatha

One of the four sons of rishi Vishvamitra.

Mahodara

Along with Trishira and Devantaka, he fought fierce battles against the vanara forces led by Angada but ultimately he was killed by Neela vanara.

Mahodara

One of the sons of Ravana. He was killed by Sugreeva.

Mainda

Son of Sushena, a vanara born from an element of the Ashwani Kumaras. His younger brother was Dvivida. Both were maternal uncles of Angada. They had obtained a boon from Brahma that no one could kill them in a battle. They fought valiantly against the rakshasa forces of Ravana.

Maka

Son of Khara. He had obtained a powerful trident from Mahadeva and with it he fought the vanara forces led by Sugreeva. After a fierce battle Maka was killed by Rama.

Mali

Son of Sukesha rakshasa and gandharvi Gramani's daughter Devavati–brother of Malyavan and Sumali. The three brothers mounted an attack against the devas. Mali was beheaded by Vishnu using His Sudarshana chakra. This had taken place before Rama's time but this past event was recalled and told by Agastya rishi to Rama.

Malyavan

Brother of Sumali and Mali–eldest of the three sons of Sukeshu. As a result of a long penance he obtained a boon for a long life and the three brothers were assigned to rule over Lanka. Later, when they attacked swarga to subdue the devas, Malyavan saw the beheading of Mali at the hands of Vishnu. Recognizing the greater strength of Vishnu, he retired to the subterranean world.

When Lanka was ruled by Kubera and then later by Ravana, Malyavan returned to the earth and advised Ravana to return Seeta to Rama but his plea fell on deaf ears.

Along with Sumali he was regarded as Ravana's maternal grandfather. He married gandharvi Narmada's daughter, Sundari, and among his sons were Virupaksha, Durmukha, and a daughter, Anata.

Mandakarni

A rishi who undertook a penance in the lake Panchasara. The devas, fearing that this rishi might usurp their place, sent five beautiful apsaras to interrupt his penance. Mandakarni was enticed and spent the rest of his life in their company. They entertained him with divine music and dances. When

Rama, Lakshmana and Seeta were passing by this spot in the early days of their forest exile, they heard this divine music but could not see anyone there. Upon inquiry old rishi Dharmabhuta related the above history and said that the apsaras continued to entertain Mandakarni rishi invisibly with their music.

Mandavi

Wife of Bharata – daughter of King Janaka's brother Kushadhwaja. Mother of Taksha and Pushkal.

Mandeha

A class of rakshasas who lived beyond the Lohita sea. Every morning, at sun rise, they fought against the sun but, not succeeding in their endeavour, they fell into water and spent the night hanging upside down from trees in the mountains.

Mandodari

Wife of Ravana—mother of Indrajit. She was the daughter of Maya danava and apsara Hema who also had two sons, Mayavi and Dundubhi.

Manibhadra

A yaksha commander of Kubera's army. In the battle between yakshas and rakshasas in Kailasa, Manibhadra fought valiantly but was overpowered by Ravana. He retired from the battlefield.

Manthara

Daughter of daitya Virochana. Indra killed her because she was getting ready to destroy the whole world. This was related to Rama by Vishvamitra to justify that it was not sinful to kill a woman under exceptional circumstances.

Manthara (Kubja)

Devoted maid of Kaikeyi. In the perceived interest of her mistress she instigated Queen Kaikeyi not to be overjoyed by the impending coronation of Rama but to think of the interest of her own son Bharata. Reminding the Queen that she had not yet availed of King Dasharatha's earlier offer to fulfil her desires, she urged Kaikeyi to ask the King to send Rama into forest exile for fourteen years and install Bharata as the Crown Prince. Although Kaikeyi at first did not consider such demands to be just, Manthara continued arguing by painting an exaggerated picture of ill-treatment which the Queen would suffer at the hands of Kausalya. Ultimately she succeeded in her evil design and Kaikeyi's demand to King Dasharatha led to Rama's exile to the forest.

Maricha

Born as a yaksha to Sunda and Tataka, Maricha, his mother and brother (Subahu) were cursed by Agastya rishi to become rakshasas. The two brothers in rakshasa form began to destroy yagnas being carried out in the forest by rishi munis. At the request of Vishvamitra, young Rama and Lakshmana accompanied the rishi to his ashram. When the rakshasa brothers appeared there, Rama killed Subahu but spared the life of Maricha, driving him to fall into the ocean far away. From that time Maricha developed great respect for and fear of Rama's divine strength. Abandoning the rakshasa ways he then established an ashram in Lanka and tried to live a righteous life.

After the death of Khara and several other rakshasa leaders, Ravana sought Maricha's help in carrying out his devilish plan of kidnapping Seeta in the belief that heart-broken and lonely Rama would then kill himself. But Maricha admonished him saying that he should not even think of confronting Rama who could destroy not only the King himself but the entire Lanka. Ravana, however, insisted on Maricha obeying his orders or else face death. Maricha preferred to meet his death at the hands of Rama than be killed by Ravana. So he agreed to carry out Ravana's plan.

He assumed the form of an unearthly golden deer and jumped about Rama's Panchavati dwelling. Seeta wanted to possess the deer as her pet and requested Rama to catch it. As Rama went after the deer, it drew him far away from their cottage. Finally, he fell to an unerring arrow of Rama. While dying Maricha regained his rakshasa form and in accordance with the preconceived plan he simulated Rama's voice and cried out, "Oh Lakshmana, Oh

Seeta". This led Lakshmana to leave Seeta alone in search of Rama. Ravana seiged the opportunity to kidnap Seeta.

Marichi

One of the mind-born sons of Brahma. He married Daksha prajapati's daughter Sambhuti. His son, the great Kashyapa rishi is considered as the progenitor of the devas and the daityas by his two wives, Aditi and Diti respectively.

Markendeya

One of the religious advisers of King Dasharatha.

Maruta

A rajarishi, disciple of rishi Samvarta. He had collected all the material required for Ashwamedha yagna which was conducted by Budha for the benefit of Ila. Narration of this early history signifying the benefits derived from Ashwamedha yagna led to King Rama conducting his own Ashwamedha yagna.

Maruta

Pavana devata or God of wind. He had once fallen for the beauty of Anjana (wife of vanara Kesari) while she was in a temporarily assumed human form. His embracing Anjana led her to give birth to the valiant and wise son Hanuman.

Marutta

Forty-nine sons of Diti were collectively known as Marutta or the winds. When Diti's sons, the daityas, were killed by the devas under the leadership of Indra, she requested her husband Kashyapa rishi to give her a son capable of killing Indra. He agreed saying that such a son would be born after an unusually long pregnancy during which she should undertake severe penances. Diti immediately commenced her penances and Indra naturally became apprehensive. So he began to cultivate Diti's goodwill by serving her during her long pregnancy. When Diti was at last pleased with Indra's services she proclaimed that her son would be his well-wisher.

Still Indra was uncertain and suspicious. Taking advantage of a lapse in Diti's penances, he entered her body and cut up the child to be born into seven pieces and each of the seven into further seven. Diti was philosophical about this dastardly act but she did not blame Indra because of his earlier services. All that she desired was that the forty-nine should achieve exalted positions. Thus they were made into forty-nine winds. (This tale was related by rishi Vishvamitra to Rama and Lakshmana as they were passing by the Kashaplava forest where in earlier times Diti had undertaken her prolonged penances.)

Matali

Charioteer of Indra. During the initial battle

with Ravana, Rama was fighting on foot while Ravana was riding in a chariot. Seeing this unequal combat, Indra asked Matali to take Indra's own chariot to Lanka so that Rama could fight as an equal. In all battles Matali acted as Rama's charioteer.

Matanga

Vanara Vali after killing rakshasa Dundubhi, flung the dead body far on the Rushyamooka mountain range. The body fell near the ashram of Matanga rishi. Some drops of impure blood from the rakshasa's body fell on the ashram thereby desecrating it. Matanga rishi then pronounced a curse that if Vali or any of his supporters ever dared to enter that forest he would be killed instantly. Sugreeva and his associates had sought refuge in that forest knowing that neither Vali nor any of his supporters would dare to go there.

Matta

Son of rakshasa Malyavan and Sundari.

Maya

Danava son of Diti. Father-in-law of Ravana.

After undertaking prolonged penances he had once pleased Brahma who gave him the knowledge and proficiency of creating exotic buildings and gardens. With this he became the architect of the danavas. He created a divine forest in which he lived with his beloved apsara Hema for a long time. Before going away Hema presented him with a daughter, Mandodari, whom eventually he gave in marriage to Ravana. On that occasion he also gave Ravana an extraordinary weapon with which Lakshmana was felled in battle. He had two sons: Mayavi and Dundubhi, both of whom were killed by the vanara King Vali.

Mayavi

Son of Maya danava–brother of Dundubhi.

On one occasion he had challenged Vali, the King of Kishkindha, and after a long drawn-out combat in an underground cavern he was killed by Vali. It was after this battle that a fatal misunderstanding arose between Vali and his brother Sugreeva.

Meghanada

Another name for Ravana's son Indrajit.

Mena

Wife of Himalaya – mother of Ganga and Uma (Parvati).

Menaka

An apsara who, while bathing in Pushkara lake, caught the eye of rishi Vishvamitra who was undertaking prolonged penances to achieve a higher status. After spending many years together, Vishvamitra suddenly realized the lapse in his austere meditation and allowed Menaka to return to swarga.

Merusavarni

A mahamuni–father of Swayamprabha who was the caretaker of an exotic forest of Hema apsara.

Mitradeva

In earlier times he had achieved the status of Varuna by conducting a rajasuya yagna. This was recalled by Rama in support of his desire for conducting a similar Rajasuya yagna.

Mitraghna

A rakshasa leader killed by Rama in the battle for Lanka.

N

Nala

Vanara son of Vishwakarma, the architect of the devas. He had inherited, from his father, the knowledge and technique of bridge-building. It was under his guidance that a bridge was built over the sea which enabled Rama and his forces to cross over to Lanka. Earlier, he had not revealed this ability of his for fear of being considered boastful. But he acknowledged it after the ocean (Mahodadhi) surrendered to Rama and said that it would allow Nala to build a bridge over it.

Nandishwara

Principal aide of Shankara. After taking over the Pushpaka vimana from Kubera, Ravana used to fly around in it all over the world. But once he had been stopped by Nandishwara from entering that part of the forest where Shankara was sporting with Parvati.

Narantaka

One of the four rakshasa commanders of Prahasta's army. In a gruesome battle his head was shattered by the stroke of a massive boulder by vanara Dvivida.

Narantaka

One of the sons of Ravana. He entered the battlefield after the death of his uncle Kumbhakarna. In the beginning he terrorised vanara forces but later, in a fierce duel, he died at the hands of Angada.

Narmada

A gandharvi whose three daughters Sundari, Ketumali and Vasuda, married Malyavan, Sumali and Mali respectively, the three sons of Sukesha rakshasa.

Nashwara

Father of Vali and Sugreeva—a King of Kishkindha.

Neela

Born from an element of Agni deva, Neela was a commander of Sugreeva's vanara army. In the battle for Lanka he fought valiantly and, after destroying rakshasa Nikumbha's chariot, he beheaded the terrible rakshasa under the wheel of his own chariot.

Nikumbha

Son of Kumbhakarna and trusted minister of Ravana. He was present at the Lankan royal court when Hanuman was brought there as a captive. Later, his mansion was set on fire by Hanuman. In the battle with Sugreeva's vanara forces he was killed by Neela.

Nikumbila

Family deity of Ravana. Rakshasi attendants guarding Seeta in Ashokavana wanted to kill Seeta, eat her flesh and then dance before this deity's temple.

Nimi

A very early ancestor of King Janaka of Mithila. The very strange story of his life was narrated by Rama to Lakshmana as follows:

In very early times King Nimi ruled over the city of Vaijayanta which was like Amaravati and had been established near the ashram of Gautama rishi. Desiring to please his ancestor King Ikshvaku, he thought of organizing a grand yagna and inviting rishi Vasishtha to officiate over it. But Vasishtha said that he could do so only after conducting a yagna of Indra. King Nimi was, however, anxious not to waste any time and performed the yagna immediately under the guidance of Gautama rishi.

Later, when Vasishtha returned from Indraloka, he was furious on learning that the King had not waited for him. So he rushed to the palace but, as it happened, King Nimi was fast asleep and did not come out. After waiting at the palace gate for some time, Vasishtha in great rage cursed that the King's body would become lifeless. When Nimi awoke and came to know of Vasishtha's fatal curse, he in turn cursed that Vasishtha's body too would become lifeless. Following these mutual curses both of them without their bodies began to live as winds.

When the assembled rishis realized that King Nimi was without a body, they conducted a grand yagna to which all the devas were also invited. Bhrugu rishi then agreed to bring back to life the King's lifeless body and the devas also agreed to grant him a boon. Nimi asked that he be allowed to stay as a wind in the eyes of all animals and birds. This wish was granted by the devas who also said that from time to time birds and animals would close their eyes so as to give him rest. All the rishis then churned the King's body and from that emerged a brilliant man who was named Mithi, Janaka or Vaideha. His illustrious descendent was King Janaka of Mithila, foster father of Seeta.

Nishakara

It was in this great rishi's ashram in the Vindhyachala mountain range that the eagle Sampati, brother of Jatayu, fell from the sky when his wings were burnt by the heat of the sun's rays. Looking into the future, the great rishi saw in his mind how, in a later age, Ravana would abduct Seeta and fly over his ashram. He therefore advised wingless Sampati to stay there and await the arrival of Rama so that he could show the vanara forces the way to Lanka where Seeta was kept a captive. He further proclaimed that when this useful information was given to the vanaras, his body would sprout new wings and he would once again be able to fly. After this event Nishakara rishi ended his earthly journey.

Nruga

A King of olden times who often donated cows to brahmanas. Among the donated cows there was one which the King's soldiers had inadvertently collected from an old brahmana who lived a very poor but righteous life. Realizing that his only cow was missing, he went around looking for it and finally located it at another brahmana's place. When he called out to the cow, she at once followed him. The other brahmana ran after him saying that the cow had been gifted to him by King Nruga. The two brahmanas then started quarrelling but not finding a way out, they went to the King's palace to seek justice. Although they waited at the palace gate for several days, the guards did not allow them to see the King. So, in anger, they cursed that the King would assume the form of a bird and live in underground pits and that he would not regain his original form until the day in a later age when Vishnu took birth as Krishna. The King then accepted his just punishment. Rama related this anecdote to Lakshmana to emphasise that a King must attend expeditiously to citizens seeking justice.

P

Panasa

Father of Sugreeva's wife Ruma. When Sugreeva assembled the vanara forces to assist Rama in locating and retrieving Seeta, the great vanara leader Panasa came down from the Pariyatra mountain range along with his large army. On the eve of the battle in Lanka, when Ravana was assessing Rama's forces, Sarma, the advance guard, described Panasa as extremely brave and willing to give his life for Rama.

Panasa

A rakshasa, who, along with Anala, Sampati and Pramati, had followed their leader Vibhishana and had defected to Rama's side. On the eve of the battle for Lanka, Panasa, assuming the form of a bird, had flown over Lanka to view arrangements made by Ravana to defend his city fort. His report to Vibhishana was conveyed to Rama who then arranged his own forces accordingly.

Panchajana

An asura leader who, along with another asura, Hayagreeva, had once lived on mount Chakravana.

There Vishnu had killed both these asuras and taken away the famed Sudarshana chakra which had been constructed by the great architect Vishwakarma. (Told by Sugreeva to his vanaras before they began the search for Seeta.)

Parashurama

An avatar of Vishnu carrying an axe (parasu). As a great brahmana warrior he went around the world twenty-one times to kill all the kshatriyas. This he did as a revenge against the sons of the Haihaya King Arjuna who had beheaded his innocent father, sage Jamadagni. When he came to know that Rama had successfully strung the mighty Shiva bow in King Janaka's court, he was more than astonished for he knew that no ordinary mortal could accomplish such a feat. He therefore came down from his abode in mount Mahendra and challenged Rama to string his own Vishnu bow. Although King Dasharatha tried to persuade Parshurama that Rama was still only a youth, Rama felt morally compelled to face the challenge. He then picked up the mighty Vishnu bow and strung it easily. Seeing this extraordinary feat Parshurama acknowledged that Rama was indeed an avtara of Vishnu for no one else would have even been able to lift the Vishnu bow. He then retired to mount Mahendra.

In early history Vishwakarma had created two divine bows. The devas gave one to Mahadeva with which he vanquished Tripurasura and gave the other to Vishnu. Later, during a confrontation between the two, Vishnu overpowered Shiva. Vishnu then gave away his mighty bow to Ruchika rishi of Bhrugu dynasty, the maternal grandfather of Parshurama. Mahadeva in turn gave away his mighty bow to King Devavrata of Videha and in later times it was inherited by King Janaka.

Parusha

One of the twelve rakshasa leaders who, along with their forces, followed their commander Khara when the latter launched an attack on Rama and Lakshmana to avenge the ill-treatment of his sister Surpanakha at their hands. Their battle was witnessed by rishis, devas, gandharvas, and other celestials who had all assembled in the sky to watch this great event. The entire rakshasa army was wiped out by Rama.

Patalaravana

Patalaravana and Kumbhodara were the sons of Malyavan's sister. He was the leader of the demons who had fled to Patala. From Brahma he had obtained a boon that he would stay alive until a blue diamond in his possession was broken into two. When the rakshasas were losing the battle of Lanka, Ravana sought his help. Realizing that Rama could not be defeated on ground, he made a tunnel from patala to Rama's camp and kidnapped both Rama and Lakshmana when all others were asleep. Later, Vibhishana, Sugreeva, Hanuman and others went through this tunnel and fought a battle against the demons. At Vibhishana's suggestion Hanuman stole the blue diamond from a secret hiding place and bit the diamond into two thus killing Patalaravana.

Paulastya (Vishravas)

Son of rishi Pulastya who was himself the son of a prajapati. He married Devavarnini, daughter of rishi Bhardawaja and they had a very righteous son whom they named Vishravana who became renowned as Kubera.

In later life, he married Kaikasi, the daughter of Sumali rakshasa. Now Kaikasi was very anxious to have children and she expressed this desire to Vishravas. But she had approached him at the wrong moment and he therefore cursed that the children born to her would have rakshasa tendencies. When she pleaded for forgiveness, Vishravas proclaimed that her youngest child would be righteous. Thus it transpired that the first two sons, Ravana and Kumbhakarna, as well as daughter Surpanakha, grew up as rakshasas but the youngest son Vibhishana was very righteous and he eventually became a great devotee of Rama. He was enthroned as the King of Lanka.

Paundraka

Son of rakshasa Nikumbha and grandson of Kumbhakarna. After the death of his father in the battle of Lanka, he took up arms against the forces of Rama and was killed.

Pishacha

After the death of commander Prahasta at the hands of Neela vanara, Ravana himself entered the battle against Rama. At that time a number of rakshasa leaders accompanied Ravana. Among them was valiant Pishacha. He fought fearlessly and gave up his life fighting for his royal master.

Plaksha

One of the counsellors/ministers of the vanara King Sugreeva of Kishkindha. Upon seeing an angry Lakshmana, Plaksha urged the King to give up his lethargy and reminded him of his earlier promise to Rama to provide all possible assistance in the search for Seeta.

Prabhava

A counsellor of the vanara King Sugreeva.

Pracheta(s)

Mother of rishi Valmiki, the celebrated poet-author of the epic Ramayana.

Pradhasa

One of the several rakshasis who were guarding Seeta while she was kept in captivity in Ashokavana by Ravana. Some of the rakshasis urged Seeta to yield to Ravana and gain happiness by marrying him. Others threatened to hurt her if she did not do so. Pradhasa went to the extreme saying that she would eat her up if she did not obey. Of course, Seeta did not swerve from the chosen path of righteousness.

Pradhasa

A rakshasa leader who, along with four others was sent by Ravana to capture Hanuman who, during his exploratory trip to Lanka in search of Seeta, had killed a number of rakshasa guards and damaged the trees in the Ashokavana. However, they were no match for the great Hanuman who killed them all.

Prahasta

Rakshasa son of Pushpotaka, sister of Ravana's mother Kaikasi. He was one of the most trusted and loyal ministers of Ravana. When Hanuman was captured during his exploratory trip to Lanka in search of Seeta and brought to the court of Ravana, it was Prahasta who interrogated the great vanara as to his identity and purpose of destroying the Ashokavana. His was among the first edifices in Lanka to be burnt down by Hanuman with his tail aflame. Prahasta remained loyal to Ravana throughout the battle against the forces of Rama. After his sons and many other rakshasa leaders were killed by the vanara army, he himself led a mighty force against the enemy. Despite fighting valiantly and killing a large number of the vanara army, he died fighting with Neela vanara.

Praheti

Brother of Heti who is regarded as the ancestor and founder of the rakshasa dynasty. Being righteous and virtuous, he spent his life in the forest and had no progeny.

Prajangha

A rakshasa chief who accompanied Kumbhakarna's sons, Kumbha and Nikumbha, when Ravana in great rage ordered them to go out and fight against the vanara army when Lanka was set on fire from all sides during the great war. Prajangha with a sharp sword rushed against Vali's son Angada but the latter uprooted a big tree and struck him on the head. Angada cut off his right arm and then beheaded him in a fierce battle.

Prajangha

A vanara chief who accompanied Hanuman and others to block the western gate of Lanka at the commencement of battle against the rakshasa forces of Ravana.

Pramatha

A rakshasa leader who had accompanied commander Khara's forces in the attack against the forest abode of Rama at Panchavati. He was killed.

Pramathi

Before the commencement of the battle in Lanka, Sarana, at the request of Ravana, had given a brief description of the various vanara leaders and their forces which had assembled there. Among these vanara leaders was Pramathi who, known to have faced an army of elephants, was anxious to uproot large trees to kill the rakshasas.

Pramati

Along with Anala, Panasa and Sampati he followed their leader Vibhishana and joined hands with the forces of Rama. Before the commencement of hostilities all four of them, assuming the form of birds, flew over Lanka to observe the deployment of Ravana's army and then passed on this information to Rama.

Praptigna

King of Magadha who was in the list of illustrious guests invited to the Ashwamedha yagna performed by King Dasharatha of Ayodhya. Rama and others were yet to be born.

Pratapana

A very fierce faced rakshasa leader who was blinded by the sharp arrows of Nala vanara at the very commencement of the battle in Lanka.

Praushthapada

A minister of the yaksha chief Kubera. In earlier times, when Ravana and his rakshasa army had attacked the yaksha forces of Kubera at Kailasa, Praushthapada had come out to fight with his mighty mace. But the rakshasas proved to be much too strong for the yakshas who were fighting righteously. Ultimately, Ravana prevailed over his brother Kubera.

Pulastya

Regarded as the son of a Prajapati, this great muni was beloved of the devas. In satyayuga he had undertaken austere meditations in rajarshi Trunabindu's ashram near holy mount Meru. Maidens of devas, nagas and apsaras often went there to enjoy themselves and in the process disturbed the single minded meditations of Pulastya. In a fit of rage he cursed that whoever he saw there would become pregnant.

Ilvila, the daughter of Trunabindu, not knowing of this curse, went there once and as soon as the great muni's sight fell on her, she developed signs of pregnancy. Her father was dismayed at this sudden change in his daughter and through his yogic vision he realized that this was due to the great muni's curse. He then went to him and requested him to accept Ilvila as his wife. Pulastya agreed to this and Ilvila served him selflessly. In due course she gave birth to a righteous son who was named Vishravas who eventually became the father of Kubera, Ravana and others.

Puloma

Daitya father of Shachi, father-in-law of Indra. When Ravana had attacked Indra's forces at Amaravati in swarga and as the battle between devas and rakshasas was in progress, Puloma took away his grandson Vijaya to 'Patala'. Later, Indra killed him along with rakshasa Anurhand when the latter had kidnapped Shachi.

Punjikasthala

An apsara who, while on her way to Brahmadeva, was seized and molested by Ravana. This greatly enraged Brahma and, later, when Ravana visited him, he ordained that in future if ever he tried to molest a woman against her will, his head would be shattered into a hundred pieces. This curse was the reason why Ravana never dared to force himself upon Seeta while she was in captivity at Ashokavana.

Punjikasthali

A renowned apsara who, because of a curse by Bruhaspati, was born as a female vanara named Anjana in the household of Kunjara vanara. In due course she grew up to be very beautiful and she eventually married vanara Kesari. Once, when she was sitting on a mountain top, a wind blew and lifted up her clothes. The wind god, Marutta, was enchanted by her uncovered body. Coming down to the mountain top he embraced her with his long limbs. Anjana was shocked that her single-minded devotion to her husband was sought to be sullied. Marutta told her that her chastity remained intact, as he had only desired her mentally. However, he foretold that she would give birth to an extremely intelligent and brave son who would be able to fly and jump just like the wind. Thus it was that Anjana gave birth to Hanuman.

Pururava (s)

Son of Ilaa and Budha. Prajapati Kardama had a son named Ila who became the King of Bahalika. By a curse of Mahadeva he had been turned into a woman named Ilaa. Later, Mahadeva's consort Uma relented a little and ordained that he would remain a male for one month and a woman for one month alternately. Much later after giving birth to Pururava(s), Ilaa expressed a desire to remain a male permanently. On the advice of Kardama and other rishis an Ashwamedha yagna was performed to propitiate Mahadeva who granted the wish; Ilaa became a male permanently. (This episode was related by Rama to Lakshmana and Bharata to underline the importance of Ashwamedha yagna before he performed such a grand yagna, himself.)

Pushkala

Son of Bharata. Towards the end of Rama's reign over Ayodhya, Pushkala and his brother Taksha, along with their father, led a mighty force against King Sailusha of Gandharva and conquered that territory. There Bharata founded two prosperous cities. Taksha was entrusted with the rule of Takshashila while Pushkala was named the King of Pushkalavati.

R

Raghu

An illustrious King of the solar dynasty and an ancestor of Rama.

Rama

The central figure for the glorification of whose virtuous life, the eternal poem Ramayana was composed. He is regarded as a supreme avatara of Vishnu who voluntarily agreed to take birth on the earth as a human in order to slay Ravana, an evil incarnate. Ravana had obtained from Brahma, a boon by which he could not be killed at the hands of devas, gandharvas, rakshasas or yakshas; in his arrogance he did not mention men whom he considered weak. Unlike Krishna, who was fully aware of his divinity and the purpose for which he had taken birth on earth, Rama lived a normal human life. In the process, he established moral and ethical standards for all human beings to follow. He is considered to be an ideal person in all respects and a universal model. Unaffected by agonies and ecstasies, pain and pleasure, happiness and unhappiness, he led a supremely righteous life in pursuit of truth and ushered in a new and enlightened era based on justice, compassion and tolerance for all. Here are the major events of his life.

He was born as the son of King Dasharatha of Ayodhya and Queen Kaushalya. He accorded to Sumitra and Kaikeyi, the two other wives of the King, the same degree of love and respect shown to his own mother. Bharata, Lakshmana and Shatrughna, the King's sons by his two other wives, adored him. Of all his four sons, however, Rama was the apple of the King's eye and the subjects of Ayodhya also loved him greatly. He grew up to be a handsome youth.

One of his earliest adventures was to go with rishi Vishvamitra to the forest and kill rakshasas Marichi and Subahu who were constantly interrupting yagnas being undertaken by the rishis. He was accompanied on this mission by his devoted brother Lakshmana. During their journey to Vishvamitra's yagna he acquired divine weapons and techniques of using them from the great rishi. On the way, Rama fought against and killed the evil demoness Tataka and then, using his divine weapons, he also killed Marichi and Subahu. After that they proceeded towards Mithila to see the great Shiva bow which was on display there on the occasion of the King Janaka's grand yagna. As they were passing by the abandoned hermitage of Gautama rishi,

Ahalya, who had been cursed to become a motionless fossil, was revived to her original glory merely when she set her eyes on Rama.

In Mithila King Janaka had announced that his daughter Seeta would be given in marriage to anyone who succeeded in stringing the mighty Shiva bow which he had inherited from his ancestors. While several suitors had failed in even lifting the mighty bow, Rama easily picked it up and broke it into two after stringing it successfully. Thus it was that the wedding of Rama and Seeta was held to the great joy of King Dasharatha and the citizens of both Ayodhya and Mithila.

On the way back to Ayodhya the wedding party was confronted by the great Parashurama who had heard of Rama's incredible feat in Mithila. He then challenged Rama to string his own Vishnu bow. Rama accomplished this easily and Parashurama retired to mount Mahendra. Rama and Seeta returned to Ayodhya triumphantly and spent many happy years together earning the admiration of all people.

King Dasharatha was now getting on in age and he decided to proclaim Rama as the Crown Prince. This announcement was welcomed by all. On the eve of the scheduled ceremony, however, Queen Kaikeyi reminded the King of his earlier promise to grant two of her wishes. The King readily agreed to grant whatever she desired. She then asked that her own son Bharata be crowned as the Crown Prince and that Rama be sent away to forest exile for fourteen years. The King was stunned and fell to the ground unconscious. When Rama was informed of these developments, his major concern was to allow his father to keep his promise. He showed neither sorrow, disappointment or hatred just as he had shown neither joy, happiness or pride when earlier he had been asked to make preparations for the morning's festivities. Accompanied by Seeta and Lakshmana he then left Ayodhya wearing the simple garb of a mendicant. The citizens of Ayodhya were greatly distressed.

Leaving the boundaries of Koshala, the trio first encountered Guha, the hunter chief, who helped them to cross the Ganga. They proceeded towards the hermitage of Bharadwaja rishi near the confluence of Ganga and Yamuna. They crossed the Yamuna and entered Chitrakoota forest where on the banks of Mandakini river they built a cottage and started their life in the forest.

Meanwhile in Ayodhya, King Dasharatha died a heart-broken father grieving for his beloved Rama. Bharata who, at that time, was away at his maternal uncle's place, was summoned in haste and informed of all the developments. He admonished his own mother and, refused to sit on the throne that belonged to Rama. He set out to meet Rama and urge him to return to Ayodhya. Rama politely declined the earnest pleas of Bharata, three Queens and various assembled rishis. He held that his prime duty was to enable his father to keep his promise. Finally, Bharata took Rama's wooden sandals saying that he would place these on the throne of Ayodhya and rule as a regent of Rama.

After the departure of the royal entourage, Rama, Lakshmana and Seeta left Chitrakoota and proceeded towards the fierce Dandaka forest where they established their residence at Panchavati. On their way there they overpowered or killed a number of evil rakshasas including Viradha. They also visited the ashrams of a number of holy rishis like Sharabhanga, Sutikshana, Agastya and Atri and obtained their blessings and supreme weapons. Sati Ansuya gave Seeta some divine ornaments and clothes which never got dirty. They also met and gained the friendship of Jatayu, the great eagle.

Once Ravana's sister Surpanakha, seeing the two brothers, instantly fell in love with them and asked them to accept her. Upon being rejected by both she tried to catch hold of Seeta but Lakshmana, at Rama's command, only cut off her nose and ears because he did not want to kill a female. Thereupon Surpanakha in terrible agony complained to her brother Khara and urged him to take revenge. This was the real beginning of animosity of Ravana towards Rama. When Khara mounted an attack on what he thought were two ordinary humans, he was killed along with his rakshasa forces. The only surviving rakshasa, Akampana, then related Rama's exploits to Ravana. Surpanakha described the incomparable beauty of Seeta.

Ravana, partly in anger and partly out of lust, decided to carry away Seeta from Panchavati to Lanka. He wanted to do this in a devious way. He instructed Maricha (see Maricha) to take the form of a deer and, gambolling before Seeta's hut, induce her in such a manner as to make Rama go in pursuit of him as a deer. He would have to drag Rama to a long distance; in Rama's absence, he (Ravana) himself would seek Seeta's hospitality in the guise of an ascetic and forcibly take her in his aerial car to Lanka. Maricha, much against his will but in fear of death at Ravana's hands — he preferred death from an arrow of Rama — acted as instructed and enabled Ravana to have his way.

Rama, who safely returned to an empty home, was deeply distressed. Initially, he vent his anger on Lakshmana but later, pacified by the latter, started on a search for Seeta. The brothers learnt from Jatayu, the Lord of Eagles, that the villain was Ravana. Kabandha, a hideous monster (see Kabandha), on recovering his original lovely male form, told them to seek the friendship of Sugreeva, the exiled brother of Vali, the Vanara King of Kishkindha, in finding out the whereabouts of Seeta. Rama redeemed Sabari, an old woman, in the Pampa region, before going to Kishkindha.

In Kishkindha Rama made friends with Sugreeva who, overcoming his initial suspicions, promised all his help in finding Seeta. The bonds of friendship were strengthened by the sagacious counsel of Hanuman. The search was resumed after the rainy season. Four search parties consisting of vanara leaders went out in four different directions. Only the party that included Hanuman and went in the southern direction succeeded in learning that Seeta was in Lanka. Hanuman, who had the capacity to fly over the sea and cover a distance of 100 yojanas (900 miles), found Seeta in Ashokavana in a distressed state. Dispelling all Seeta's fears and suspicions, Hanuman handed over the signet ring given to him by Rama and returned to Kishkindha with the crest-jewel handed over to him by Seeta.

Rama and the vanaras, billions of them, were faced with the problem of crossing the sea. Thanks to Nala, the celestial architect, a bridge was built in five days and the 'army' found itself on the outskirts of Lanka. Rama ordered the forces to form themselves in battle array.

Rama led the war which raged day and night, over several days. There were three occasions when Rama, along with Lakshmana, fell unconscious and were helped to regain consciousness. All these happened when Indrajit fought with the brothers. The climax of the war was the fight between Rama and Ravana.

Ravana initially pierced the chest of Lakshmana with a javelin which depressed Rama. Recovering, Rama drove Ravana to seek his safety and the weak Lakshmana continued to insist on Rama to do away with the wily Rakshasa King.

Indra sent a chariot along with a charioteer, Matali by name, to Rama by way of helping him. At one stage, Ravana's charioteer drove away from the scene when he found that Ravana was struggling to string his bow. Ravana, with his characteristic aplomb, rebuked him and asked the charioteer to take him back to the battlefield.

Rama, energised by intoning the hymn to the Sun taught by Agastya, faced Ravana. Both locked themselves in a battle which even Valmiki, master of the simile, found difficult to describe. He contented himself by saying: "The Sky is like the sky and like nothing else, and the ocean can be compared only to the ocean. Similarly, in the fight between Rama and Ravana, without a parallel, like Rama and Ravana themselves."

Rama found to his amazement that even as he cut off one head of Ravana another came in its place, and thus found himself at least a hundred heads. At the suggestion of Matali, Rama let off the

Brahmastra and the arrow, going with lightning speed, pierced the heart of Ravana. The blood-stained arrow, after this marvellous deed, returned back to Rama's quiver.

His misson accomplished, everyone looked forward to Rama rejoicing in his re-union with Seeta. This was not to be, Rama insisted on Seeta going through a fire ordeal, demonstrating merely her chastity. The Fire-God, bearing Seeta in his hands, and emerging from the blaze, told Rama: "Accept her, O Raghava, she is pure-hearted and wholly without stain. I command you to do so. I will not bear a word against her."

Seeta's woes did not end with this fire ordeal. After his coronation in Ayodhya, Rama asked Lakshmana to leave a pregnant Seeta in the forest, when he heard a loose talk among his people about Seeta's stay in Lanka. Rama saw Seeta again in Valmiki's hermitage where Seeta lived and gave birth to twins, Lava and Kusa. When Rama wanted her to prove her 'innocence' once again in the royal assembly, Seeta prayed to the Mother Goddess to take her back to her bosom. From earth she came and to earth she returned. Such was Seeta, purer than purity itself, as is said of her.

Even when he repudiated Seeta, Rama stuck to Dharma; in the case of Seeta, he followed Raja Dharma.

A popular Sanskrit saying sums up Rama as the very image of Dharma — Ramo vigrahevaan dharmah. He was the very soul of righteousness, a votary of truth and unrivalled in valour.

Rambha

A vanara leader who put his force of eleven thousand vanaras under the command of Sugreeva in the task of locating and retrieving Seeta.

Rambhaa

Daughter of Kashyapa prajapati. She was considered to be one of the most beautiful apsarases of swarga and a favourite of Indra. Once, when Ravana was going to mount Kailash, he encountered her while she was on her way to meet her beloved Nalakubera, son of Kubera. Upon seeing her beautiful form, Ravana could not control his passion and although Rambhaa pleaded that she was like his daughter-in-law, he forced himself upon her. When Nalakubera came to know of this he pronounced a curse upon Ravana that if ever he forced himself upon an unwilling woman, his head would crack into seven pieces. Because of this curse Ravana never dared to touch Seeta while she was in his captivity in Lanka.

Rashmiketu

One of the rakshasa chiefs whose abode in Lanka was reduced to ashes by Hanuman jumping from one building to another after his tail was set on fire. He was beheaded by Rama in the battle for Lanka.

Rashtravardhana

One of the eight ministers of King Dasharatha of Ayodhya.

Renuka

Mother of Parashurama- wife of rishi Jamadagni.

Romapada

A King of Angadesha who was a great friend of Dasharatha. His daughter Shanta was married to rishi Rishyashrunga.

Rovasha

A rakshasa chief whose abode in Lanka was destroyed by fire when Hanuman jumped all over the city with his burning tail.

Ruchika

Husband of rishi Vishvamitra's sister Satyavati — father of sage Jamadagni and grand father of Parashurama.

Ruchika

A muni of ancient times who gave away Shunashepa, second of his three sons, to King

Ambrisha whose sacred beast had been stolen and without which the King could not complete his yagna. (See Ambarisha and Sunahshepa)

Rudhirashana

A rakshasa chief and bodyguard of Khara who was killed by Rama during the fierce battle in Dandakaranya forest where Khara had gone along with his force of fourteen thousand rakshasas to take revenge against Rama and Lakshmana who had disfigured his sister Surpanakha.

Ruksharajasa

Father of Vali and Sugreeva. He was a great King of Kishakindha.

Ruma

Wife of vanara King Sugreeva and daughter of vanara Panasa. Vali, after defeating Sugreeva and exiling him to a mountain-top, kept Ruma with him. Later, when Sugreeva, with the help of Rama, killed Vali and regained the throne of Kishkindha, Ruma became the Queen and enjoyed that status for a long time.

Rumpana

When Sugreeva assembled all his forces to help Rama, his friend and saviour, Rumpana, came there with his clan of numerous vanaras.

Rushabha

A vanara chief whose force constituted the main element of the right wing of Rama's army when he prepared to attack Ravana's Lanka.

Rishyashrunga

A rishi who married Shanta, daughter of King Romapada of Angadesha who was a great friend of King Dasharatha. He officiated at the yagna conducted by King Dasharatha for progeny.

It is said that it rained in any place he visited. He was invited to kingdoms which suffered from droughts.

S

Sachi

Consort of Indra – daughter of Puloma rakshasa. In her youth she had been kidnapped by Anurhada rakshasa but Indra killed him and brought Sachi to Amaravati. This was recalled by Rama while relating to Sugreeva how Ravana had kidnapped Seeta and how he too would meet the same fate.

Sagara

An early ancestor of Rama. His great grandson Bhagiratha persuaded Ganga to fall to earth and flow over the ashes of his grand uncles who were burnt to ashes from the wrath of Kapila muni. This early history was related by Vishvamitra rishi to Rama and Lakshmana.

Sahastramukha

He was a daitya ruler of Trilokapuri. He had a thousand heads and two thousand hands. He was married to Indumukhi, daughter of Patalaravana. Their sons were Vajrabahu and Chandragupta. The former was killed by Subramanya.

Having obtained a boon from Brahma that he would not be killed by anyone except a woman, he conquered all the three worlds. When he violated Chanchalakshmi, a vidyadhara woman, she pronounced a curse that he would be killed by Lakshmidevi.

Once, after the coronation of Rama, Chandragupta abducted Sugreeva's daughter (Vibhishana's daughter-in-law). Rama, along with others, then entered into a battle with Sahastramukha. When during the fight Angada was about to be overpowered by Chandragupta, a celestial voice was heard saying that Chandragupta could not be killed as long as his wife Padmavati was reciting 'Brahmamantra'. Then Hanuman, at the suggestion of Vibhishana, went to the women's quarters and caused great confusion as a result of which Padmavati stopped her recitation of 'Brahmamantra'. Angada then killed Chandragupta and finally Sahastramukha was beheaded by Lakshmidevi.

Salakalkanta

Wife of an elderly rakshasa Vidyutakesha. She was the daughter of Sandhya and mother of Sukesha rakshasa.

Sampati

One of the four spies of Vibhishana. Along with

Anala, Panasa and Pramati, he had taken the form of a bird and flown over Lanka to study the size and deployment of Ravana's army.

Sampati

Elder brother of Jatayu. In the Ramayana these two birds, who were descendants of Kashyapa Prajapati and Vinata, are depicted as vultures. In their youth the two brothers contested as to who could fly higher. Jatayu flew so high that his wings got scorched by the heat of the sun. In order to protect his younger brother, Sampati flew over him to provide shade. Jatayu was thus saved but Sampati's wings got completely burnt and he fell down on Vindhya mountain near the hermitage of Nishakara rishi. The great rishi arranged to have him fed and assured him that in future he would be instrumental in aiding Rama and that at that time new wings would sprout from his body.

After Nishakara muni ended his earthly life, Sampati in despondence often thought of ending his life too but the prospect of helping Rama kept him alive. Finally, when Sugreeva and other vanaras came that way he was able to tell them that earlier he had seen Ravana, the demon King of Lanka, abducting Seeta. With his divine vision he could see that Seeta was being kept in captivity in Ashokavana in Lanka. At that moment new wings sprouted from his body. Regaining his vigour, he flew away into the sky. The delighted vanaras then returned to Kishakindha to convey this news to Rama.

Samunnata

One of the four commanders of rakshasa Prahasta's army. In the battle for Lanka, vanara Durmukha crushed him to death with a blow of a big tree.

Sandhya

Mother of Salakalkanta who was the wife of rakshasa Vidyutakesha.

Sannadana

One of the vanara chiefs. He had once fought against Indra and had come out unscathed.

Sanvarta

Brother of Brahaspati, the preceptor of the devas. While officiating at a yagna being conducted by King Marutta, Ravana came there and challenged the King to a fight. When the King was getting ready to fight, Sanvarta rishi calmed him and urged him to continue the yagna.

Sanyodhakautaka

A yaksha commander who was sent by Kubera to fight against the forces of Ravana when the latter had launched an attack against the yakshas. He fought a pitched battle against Maricha rakshasa but could not vanquish him and retired from the battlefield.

Saptajana

A group of seven rishis. The forest which had grown up at the place where these rishis had performed severe penances, was so thick that it could not be penetrated even by birds. The history of this thicket was related to Rama by Sugreeva while they were going to Kishakindha to challenge Vali to a fight.

Sarama

One of the several rakshasis who guarded Seeta in Ashokavana while she was kept there in captivity. Once Ravana came there and through his power of illusion, produced the head of Rama telling Seeta that as he had already killed her husband, she should agree to become his Queen. At this Seeta broke down in despair. After the departure of Ravana, Sarama who had taken kindly to Seeta and had developed fondness for her, consoled her saying that Rama was quite well and that in fact along with the army of vanaras he had already crossed the sea and landed in Lanka. Thus Seeta's courage was restored.

Sarana

A rakshasa chief who, along with Shuka, was asked by Ravana to assess the nature, size and strength of the vanara forces which had landed in Lanka. Accordingly, the two flew over Rama's camp in disguise. Vibhishana spotted them and, catching them, brought them to Rama for punishment. But Rama proclaimed that it was unfair to kill unarmed and captive enemy messengers. After being released by Rama, they returned to Lanka and, describing the immense vanara army, urged Ravana not to battle with Rama. But their sincere advice was not accepted by Ravana.

Sarapasya

One of the rakshasa chiefs who had accompanied commander Khara to confront Rama at Panchavati and take revenge for the suffering inflicted upon Surpanakha. But he, along with some fourteen thousand rakshasas, was killed by Rama.

Sarma

Wife of Vibhishana. She was the daughter of gandharva Sailusha. She was born on the shore of Manasarovar lake. She gave birth to a daughter, Kala.

Savitra

One of the eight vasus. When the rakshasas under the leadership of Ravana launched a full-scale attack against Indrapuri, the capital of Indra, Savitra fought valiantly and, in the process, killed Sumali, father-in-law of Ravana.

Seeta (Janaki)

The immaculate heroine of the Ramayana. She was the wife of Rama and foster daughter of Janaka.

Their marriage was brought about by Rishi Vishvamitra who took the brothers, Rama and Lakshmana, to Mithila after they had helped the rishi in getting rid of Maricha and Subahu, the spoilers of the sacrifice he was performing. The marriage took place after Rama had lifted and strung Shiva's bow — a feat never done by the earlier suitors of Seeta. At the wedding, when Rama and Seeta were seated before the holy fire, Janaka told Rama: "This Seeta, my daughter, will be your partner in the Dharmic life. Receive her — may all good attend you! Take her by the hand. Devoted to her lord, she will be fortunate, always following you like a shadow." As if to confirm Janaka's words, Seeta insisted upon going to the forest along with Rama when the latter, in order to fulfill a promise of his father made to Kaikeyi, agreed to go into exile for fourteen years. Seeta, besides being a 'pativrata' (devoted to her husband) had a stubborn will. That she had a mind of her own was clear when she told Rama: "What was my father about — when he chose you, a woman in man's guise for his Son-in-law...?"

Before entering the Dandakaranya, Seeta was received by Atri and Anasuya in their cottage. She was not only praised by Anasuya for her devotion to her husband, but was given celestial unguents and ornaments. Anasuya said among other things: "...women like you, possessed of virtue have an abiding place in heaven."

In the Dandaka forest, Rama assured the sages his protection from the harassment of the rakshasas. Later, Seeta turned a counsellor to Rama. She reminded him of his offer of protection to the hermits and said that infliction of cruelty without provocation was one of the three 'weaknesses' of men – the other two being telling a lie and consorting with another man's wife. Rama replied that "he had a duty as the scion of royal dynasty to save the oppressed."

A turning-point in the epic story came when Seeta was carried away by Ravana from Panchavati to Lanka. As if by forethought, Seeta dropped some clothes and ornaments from the aerial car in which she was being taken to Lanka.

In Lanka, Seeta suffered not only the pangs of separation from Rama but the harassment of the rakshasis surrounding her at the Ashokavana. In repulsing the advances of Ravana, she was resolute. From that depressed state of mind, she was lifted up a little when Hanuman visited her and gave her the signet ring of Rama. She felt assured that it would not be long before she rejoined her adored and beloved spouse. What she expected did happen but she had to go through a fire ordeal before she could re-join Rama.

She had a happy time during and after the coronation of Rama. But her misfortune never left her free to enjoy a life of ease and felicity. Influenced by some loose talk by the city-folk about her long captivity in Lanka, Rama asked Lakshmana to leave her in the forest again. In the forest, she lived in the hermitage of Valmiki. She gave birth to twins — Lava and Kusha. When the children took their father back to her, she did not choose to live any longer. When Rama wanted her to 'prove her innocence', she appealed to the Mother Earth to take her to her bosom — from earth, back to earth.

There is a popular saying in Sanskrit that 'Seeta's story is great'. It was certainly great but she was also fated to undergo much misery. She was a woman of great virtue and remains the ideal for all times.

Shabala

Another name for Vasishta rishi's cow Kamadhenu or Hemadhenu which fulfilled all the desires of the great rishi.

Shabari

A sanyasi woman of the hunter tribe who lived in the ashram of Matanga muni serving the great muni and his disciples. When Rama and Lakshmana passed by that ashram, she served them with reverence and then attained salvation.

In an earlier period she was Malini , daughter of King Chitrakavacha. Because of a misdemeanour her husband Vitihotra cursed that she be born as a hunter woman. Later, he relented and said that she would regain her original form after being blessed by Rama. Thus it was that, after seeing Rama, she got transformed as Malini, and her former husband took her to Gandharvaloka.

Shaibya

A King in early history who was willing to give up his life in order to keep his promise. This was recalled by Queen Kaikeyi when King Dasharatha was hesitating to keep the promise he had given her earlier.

Shailesha

Father of Vibhishana's wife. He ruled over the Kingdom of Gandharva on the banks of river Sindhu. Towards the end of Rama's reign his army led by Bharata and his sons, Taksha and Pushkala, conquered the Gandharva Kingdom.

Shamba

Asura King of Vaijyanta. He was also called Timidhwaja. It was during a battle with this asura that King Dasharatha had been felled and his life had been saved by Queen Kaikeyi acting as his charioteer. In return the King promised to fulfil two wishes of his Queen. Kaikeyi said that she would avail of some other occasion to ask for the favours. It was on the basis of this episode that Kaikeyi, on the eve of Rama's coronation, asked King Dasharatha to install her own son Bharata on the throne of

Ayodhya and banish Rama to the forest for fourteen years.

Shambhu

Son of Ravana's sister Surpanakha. During the forest exile of Rama, Lakshmana and Seeta, this rakshasa took the form of an ebony tree to admire closely the beauty of Seeta. When Lakshmana felled this tree to collect wood for constructing their hut, Shambhu was killed.

Shambuka

Towards the end of Rama's reign, a brahmana once came to the King lamenting that his young child, although in perfect health, had died of no known reason. He held the King responsible for such an unjust occurrence. Narada muni, who happened to be there, advised Rama that some wrongful deed was being perpetrated somewhere in his kingdom and that it was the king's responsibility to stop it at once. Rama then flew over the Kingdom in Pushpaka vimana. He saw a man undertaking severe penances hanging upside down from the branch of a tall tree near the ashram of Agastya rishi. When asked, the man said that he was Shambuka, a shudra who wanted to gain the kingdom of the devas. Considering his penance (by a shudra) to be unjust, Rama killed him on the spot. At that very instance, the brahmana's child got back its life.

Sharabha

A vanara chief living in Shalveya mountain range. He contributed a large force to Sugreeva's army.

Sharabhanga

After killing Viradha rakshasa, Rama, along with Lakshmana and Seeta, approached the ashram of the great Sharabhanga rishi who, by his austerities and penances, had earned the right to reside in Brahmaloka. Indra himself had come down in all his majesty to take this rishi to Brahmaloka. But Indra, upon seeing Rama, went back saying that it would not be proper to meet Rama in this state. Sharabhanga rishi then explained to Rama that he did not wish to go to Brahmaloka without having his darshan. After paying respectful homage to Rama he then advised the trio to proceed towards the ashram of Sutikshana and showed them the way. He then entered the holy fire and achieved Brahmaloka.

Sharari

Another vanara chief who formed a part of the above team.

Shardula

Before Rama and his army had built a bridge to cross over to Lanka, Shardula, a rakshasa spy, happened to see this vanara force. He quickly returned to Lanka and alerted Ravana about what he had seen so that the King could take appropriate counter measures.

Shatabala

A vanara commander who was sent by Sugreeva in the norther direction to search for Seeta but he returned without success after a month.

Shatabali

A vanara chief who contributed a large force to Sugreeva's army. He was a devotee of Suryanarayana.

Shatahrada

Mother of Viradha rakshasa — wife of Java.

Shatananda

Son of Gautama rishi and Ahalya. He was one of the priests who officiated at the yagna conducted by King Janaka. Later, he acted as the high priest at the marriage ceremony of Rama and Seeta.

Shatrughna

Younger brother of Lakshmana — son of King Dasharatha and Queen Sumitra. Although Lakshmana and Shatrughna were born of the same mother, he was more closely associated with Bharata. He married Shrutakirti, daughter of King Janaka's brother, Kushadhwaja, and had two sons, Subahu and Shurasena.

Upon returning to Ayodhya from his maternal uncle's place, along with Bharata, he came to know about Rama's decision to accept forest exile. When he learnt that Kaikeyi's maid Manthara was behind this evil scheme, he was prepared to kill her but was stopped from doing so by Bharata.

After the coronation of Rama as the King of Ayodhya, Shatrughna volunteered to overpower Lavanasura who was harassing Chyavana and other rishis. He then led a large army and marched towards the palace of the great asura leader. Knowing that the asura could not be killed so long as he possessed a special arrow given to him by Shiva, he waited until the day the asura king went hunting without the special arrow. In his absence he got the special arrow and then killed Lavanasura in a battle. He then founded the city of Madhupuri (Mathura of today) and installed his son Subahu to rule over it. His life came to an end along with those of Rama and Bharata (Lakshmana having died earlier).

Shonitaksha

This rakshasa and his brother Yupaksha fought a night battle against Angada and his vanara army. They were under the command of Kumbhakarna's sons, Kumbha and Nikumbha. Ultimately, he was killed by Dvivida vanara.

Shraavana

Only son of a brahmana couple who had become

old and blind. He was their only support. One night he had gone to the river to fetch water for his old parents.

At that time, prince Dasharatha, in the prime of his youth, was practising the art of shooting at an object without seeing but by hearing the sound emanating from the target. Hearing the sound of water entering Shraavana's pot, he shot a deadly arrow at it thinking that it was some wild animal. But he was aghast at hearing a human cry of agony. Approaching the river bank he realized the magnitude of his misadventure but by then it was too late. Before dying Shraavana requested the prince to take care of his dependant parents. With a heavy heart and in fear Dasharatha admitted to the old couple the grave mistake he had committed. In great despair the couple decided to give up their lives too. But before dying the old man said that the sin of killing a brahmana would not stick to the prince as, he had killed a brahmana through error. However, he would have to suffer the pain of separation from his own son before dying.

This happened many years later after Rama had gone to the forest. King Dasharatha, while on his deathbed related this episode from his life to Queen Kaushalya.

Shrutakirti

Wife of Shatrughna — daughter of King

Janaka's younger brother Kushadhwaja. They had two sons: Taksha and Pushkala

Shuka

A minister of Kubera who led an army of yakshas against the invading force of Ravana but he was overpowered by the rakshasas.

Shuka

A rakshasa, who, along with Sarana, flew over the vanara forces to assess their strength but was detected and caught by Vibhishana. He was, however, pardoned by Rama as he carried no arms.

Shunaka

Youngest of three sons of Ruchika rishi – younger brother of Shunakshepa. His mother refused to part with him when King Ambarisha offered to buy him to replace the lost sacrificial animal which had been selected for his yagna.

Shunakshepa

Second of the three sons of Ruchika rishi. Once King Ambrisha requested the rishi to sell him one of his three sons to replace the lost sacrificial animal required for the completion of his yagna. Ruchika rishi refused to give away his eldest son and the mother of the boys refused to part with the youngest. So it was Shunakshepa who was given to the King.

Later his life was saved by Vishvamitra rishi. The rishi taught the boy two hymns in praise of Indra. Indra was pleased and granted the boy a long life.

Shura

Father of Queen Sumitra. Maternal grandfather of Lakshmana and Shatrughna.

Shuragulma

A vanara chief who was a part of the team sent by Sugreeva in search of Seeta in the southern direction under the leadership of Angada.

Shveta

A great rishi whom the asura Andhaka tried to slay. But Shankara, in order to protect his devotee, kicked the asura and killed him. It was in this manner that Rama killed Khara rakshasa in Dandakaranya.

Shveta

One of the many vanara commanders who was renowned in all the three worlds for his great valour and intellect.

Shveta

King of Vidarbha in early history. After ruling over his Kingdom for a long time, he retired to the forest and gained Brahmaloka as a result of his severe penance. But even there he was afflicted with hunger and thirst because in his life as a King he had not given alms to brahmanas. It was, therefore, ordained that his hunger and thirst could be quenched only by consuming his own flesh. Ultimately, he got redemption at the hands of Agastya rishi. In gratitude the King gave a divine ornament to Agastya who in turn later presented it to Rama.

Shyenagami

One of the commanders of the fourteen thousand strong rakshasa force of Khara. Along with other rakshasas he was killed by Rama.

Shyeni

Mother of the great bird Jatayu – wife of Aruna.

Siddharta

One of the favourite ministers of King Dasharatha. When Queen Kaikeyi demanded that Rama be sent into exile for fourteen years, Siddharta tried to persuade her not to insist on such an unreasonable demand. But all his attempts were of no avail. Later, after the death of King Dasharatha, he along with others, went to fetch Bharata and Shatrughna from their maternal uncle's place.

Simhika

A ferocious rakshasi who lived under the sea which Hanuman had to cross on his way to Lanka in his search for Seeta. When she saw Hanuman flying across the sea, she caught hold of his shadow and at once Hanuman's progress was stopped. She then came out of the sea and, making her body grow to an immense size, opened her mouth to swallow Hanuman. The clever vanara then reduced his size greatly and entered the rakshasi's body through her wide open mouth. He then killed her by tearing her stomach and then resumed his flight.

Sthulaksha

One of the several commanders of Khara rakshasa who confronted Rama and was killed along with Mahakapala and Pramathi.

Sthulashira

A sage who, upon being frightened by demon Kabandha, cursed him that he would remain in an ugly body until his hands were cut off by Rama.

Subahu

Brother of rakshasa Maricha. When the rakshasas attempted to interrupt and destroy the yagna being conducted by Vishvamitra rishi, he along with his brother was killed by Rama.

Sudama

Minister of King Janaka of Mithila who was asked to invite King Dasharatha of Ayodhya to come to Mithilanagari to attend the swayamvara of princess Seeta.

Sudhanva

King of Sankashya which was adjacent to King Janaka's Mithilapuri. Once Sudhanva sent an ultimatum to Janaka that either he should give him princess Seeta together with the famous 'Shiva dhanusha' or face him in battle. King Janaka accepted the challenge and in the ensuing battle Sudhanva was killed and his capital Sankashya was captured. Janaka's younger brother, Kushadhwaja, was then coronated as the King of Shankashya.

Sugreeva

As the chief of the vanara sena, he was the principal ally of Rama in the battle against Ravana. He was the younger brother of Vali, the King of Kishakindha, whom he served diligently. As a result of a grave misunderstanding between the two, however, he along with his adviser Hanuman, was expelled from the Kingdom. Vali also took his dear wife Rama. Sugreeva then took refuge in mount Rushyamooka where he knew Vali could not come due to a curse cast on him by Matanga rishi. There he encountered Rama and Lakshmana wandering in the forest in the garb of sanyasis. In fact, Rama wanted to meet Sugreeva who, according to giant

Kabandha, would provide him with valuable clues as to the whereabouts of Seeta. With the help of Hanuman, he established friendship with Rama. An understanding was reached between them, that Rama would kill Vali, and restore Kishakindha to him. In return Sugreeva would provide all assistance to Rama in finding and getting back Seeta.

Sugreeva recalled how a few days earlier he had seen a big rakshasa named Ravana flying through the air holding a pretty maiden who kept on crying out “Hey Rama! Hey Lakshmana!”. Seeing the vanaras sitting by the mountain she then threw towards them her scarf and a few of her ornaments. When the ornaments were displayed to Rama he was convinced that Seeta had indeed been taken away by Ravana in a southern direction. Sugreeva then assured Rama that his forces would help locate Seeta.

After receiving an assurance that Rama would kill Vali, Sugreeva went to the outskirts of Kishkindhanagari and challenged Vali to a fight. In the ensuing duel both the brothers looked so much alike that Rama could not first identify Sugreeva. Later, at the suggestion of Rama, Sugreeva wore a flower garland around his neck and invited Vali for a return bout. This time Rama shot an arrow aimed at Vali and killed him. Sugreeva was then coronated as the King of Kishakindha and reunited with his beloved wife Rama.

Now Sugreeva asked his army commander Nila to assemble all the vanaras for the battle. First he sent scouts to different places to locate Seeta. Hanuman went towards Lanka. After Hanuman confirmed that he had spotted Seeta in Ashokavana in Lanka, Sugreeva asked Nila and the vanara forces to build a bridge across the sea so that they could attack Ravana's army and enable Rama to retrieve Seeta.

In the war against the Lankan rakshasa army, Sugreeva fought valiantly and killed, among others, Kumbhakarna's son Kumbha, Ravana's commander Virupaksha and Mahodara. He removed Lakshmana from the battlefield when the latter had fallen unconscious.

After the end of the war he accompanied Rama to Ayodhya where he was put in charge of the army. Following Rama's death, he too gave up his life and Angada was crowned as the King of Kishakindha.

Suhotra

A vanara chief who had accompanied Hanuman, Angada and others in search of Seeta.

Suketu

A yaksha who pleased Brahma and obtained a boon by which he got a daughter named Tataka.

Sumali

Maternal grandfather of Ravana, father of Ravana's mother Kaikasi, brother of Malyavan and Mali, husband of Ketumali. He was killed by Indra's son Jayanta when Indrajit attacked Indraloka.

Sumati

King of Vishalanagari where rishi Vishvamitra, along with Rama and Lakshmana, had rested for a night while on their way to Mithila. He was a descendent of King Ikshvaku.

Sumati

One of the two wives of King Sagara of Ayodhya (the other being Keshini). She was the daughter of muni Arishthanemi and sister of Garuda. Following the boon given to King Sagara by Bhrugu rishi, she gave birth to sixty thousand valiant sons all of whom were burnt to death by the wrath of Kapila muni; they were on a search for the horse which had been taken away by Indra in the guise of a rakshasi. This episode was narrated by Vishvamitra while recalling the glories of the early ancestors of Rama.

Sumitra

One of the three wives of King Dasharatha – mother of Lakshmana and Shatrughna.

Sunayana

Wife of King Janaka of Mithila. She brought up Seeta.

Sunda

Sunda and Upasunda were two cruel asura brothers—sons of Jambasura. After performing severe penances they obtained a boon from Brahma according to which they could not be killed by anyone until they killed themselves mutually. Having secured this boon they became extremely arrogant and conquered all the three worlds. Finally, Brahma caused an exquisitely beautiful apsara named Tilottama who danced before them causing jealousy between themselves. They fought against each other over her and both died. Sunda married rakshasi Tataka – they had two sons, Subahu and Maricha.

Sundari

Wife of Malyavan — mother of Virupaksha, Duramukha, etc

Suparshva

Son of Garudaraja Sampati who had seen Ravana carrying away Seeta and who related this to his father who in turn narrated this to Angada and other vanaras.

Suparshva

One of the ministers of Ravana. When Ravana was preparing to kill Seeta to avenge the death of his dear son Indrajit, it was Suparshva who convinced him not to commit the sin of killing a woman but instead get ready to kill Rama in battle.

Supraleha

One of the two wives of prajapati Krushashva (the other being Jaya). She had given several divine weapons to muni Vishvamitra. This episode was recalled by Maharshi Vasishtha while trying to convince Dasharatha of Vishvamitra's prowess. The King out of love for his sons, had shown reluctance to send Rama and Lakshmana to accompany Vishvamitra to get rid of the rakshasas harassing the rishis.

Surasa

When the devas and the rishis wanted to test the strength and ability of Hanuman, they asked nagamata Surasa to hinder his progress while he was jumping over the ocean to reach Lanka. Surasa opened her mouth and challenged Hanuman to enter it because she had obtained a boon according to which no one could cross the ocean without entering her mouth. As Hanuman enlarged the size of his body, Surasa opened her mouth even wider. Suddenly, Hanuman reduced the size of his body and made it as small as a thumb and flew in and out of her mouth before she could close it. Thus, having fulfilled Surasa's condition, he continued his flight after receiving Surasa's blessings. Surasa's son was named Kanka.

Surashtra

One of the eight ministers of King Dasharatha.

Surpanakha

Rakshasi daughter of Paulastya (Vishravas) and Raka. Sister of Ravana and Khara. Once, while wandering in the forest, she saw Rama and attracted by his good looks, she asked him to marry her. Rama stated that Seeta was his one and only wife. Hearing this she rushed towards Seeta wanting to kill her. Rama then asked Lakshmana to tackle her. Not wanting to kill a woman, Lakshmana merely cut off her nose and ears. With a bleeding face Surpanakha went to her brother Khara who was camping nearby, and urged him to kill the two brothers. In the ensuing battle Khara was killed together with many other rakshasas. She then returned to Lanka and described to Ravana the extraordinary beauty of Seeta so that Ravana's passions would be aroused. Later, she married Vidyujivha and had a son Shambhu.

Suryabhanu

Gatekeeper of Kubera who tried to prevent Ravana from entering Kubera's palace but Ravana fought with him and killed him.

Suryodhakantaka

A commander of Kubera's army. During a battle with Ravana's forces he caused serious injury to Maricha but, when the latter regained consciousness and returned with a large force of rakshasas, Suryodhakantaka ran away from the battlefield.

Sushena

Father of Tara, the wife of Vali, Son of vanara Dharna. He led the mission in the westerly direction in search of Seeta. In the battle against the Lankan rakshasas, he fought valiantly and killed Vidyumali and others. When Lakshmana fell unconscious in the battle, Sushena asked Hanuman to fly to a Himalayan mount full of medicinal herbs and bring those herbs; Vishalyakarni, Sandhani, Savarnyakarni and Sanjivani. When Hanuman could not identify the herbs, he brought back the whole mountain peak. Sushena then extracted the needed herbs and made a juice which revived Lakshmana. Sushena attended the coronation of Rama.

Sutikshana

A rishi whose ashram was visited by Rama, Seeta and Lakshmana during their forest exile and who showed them the way to Agastya muni's ashram.

Suyagna

Son of rishi Vashistha. When Rama, Seeta and Lakshmana were preparing to go into exile, Rama gave away many of Seeta's jewels and precious belongings to Suyagna.

Svayamprabha

Daughter of muni Merusavarni and companion

of Hema apsara. She was guarding the Rukshabila cave belonging to Hema apsara. When Hanuman, Angada and other vanaras entered the cave in search of Seeta, it was Swayamprabha, the old tapasvi, who helped them to get out of the cave and then showed them the way to the southern ocean leading towards Lanka.

T

Taksha

Son of Rama's brother Bharata — brother of Pushkala. At the insistence of Rama, Bharata and his sons led an army to conquer the gandharva Kingdom of King Shailesha. After killing numerous gandharvas and conquering the land, Bharata installed Taksha on the throne of Takshashila and Pushkala on the throne of Pushkalavati.

Tamana

In the battle between the vanara's sena and the rakshasas in Lanka, Tamana rakshasa had fought against Gaja vanara.

Tamburu

A gandharva who, following a curse by Kubera, turned into Viradha, a rakshasa, and was killed by Rama and Lakshmana in Dandakaranya.

Tar

When Vishnu decided to take birth as Rama to

vanquish Ravana, Brahma requested various devas to produce valiant vanaras from their respective elements. Guru Brahaspati produced the intelligent vanara named Tar. He became the father of Sugreeva's wife Ruma.

Tara

Wife of Vali – daughter of Sushena vanara – mother of Angada. She was a fine judge of character. She tried in vain to dissuade Vali from accepting a challenge from Sugreeva for a return fight saying that Sugreeva must have received an assurance of help from Rama.

T[illegible]

A vanara sena chief who, along with Hanuman and others, guarded the western gate of Ravana's palace when Rama began his fight against the Lankan forces.

Tataka

An evil yakshini who was the wife of Sunda and mother of Maricha. Suketu rakshasa, after undertaking severe penances, had obtained her as a daughter from Brahma. She had the strength of a thousand elephants and could assume various forms. Following a curse by Agastya, both Tataka and Maricha assumed rakshasa form. Tataka kept on spoiling the yagnas of Agastya and other rishis residing in the area which lay in the path of Vishvamitra, Rama and Lakshmana. Vishvamitra then asked Rama to kill the evil rakshasi even though she was a female. When attacked by Tataka, Rama cut off her arms and Lakshmana severed her nose and ears. Even then she kept on attacking them. Finally Rama killed her and earned the gratitude of all the rishis.

Timidhwaja (Shambarasura)

Asura ruler of Vaijayantanagara, the capital of Dandakaranya, in the south. In a battle between the devas and the asuras, King Dasharatha, fighting on the side of the devas, was seriously injured by this asura. Queen Kaikeyi saved her husband by taking his chariot out of the danger zone. Being pleased with her for saving his life, King Dasharatha offered to fulfil two of her wishes. Years later, Kaikeyi reminded the King of this and asked him to coronate her son Bharata as the Crown Prince of Ayodhya and exile Rama to the forest for fourteen years.

Trambaka

A rishi who gave a divine weapon (Shula) to Lavanasura with which he could defeat any enemy. Shatrughna killed him when the evil asura was without his Shula.

Trijata

A poor brahmana of Ayodhya who was struggling to maintain his family. When his wife came to know that Rama was giving away all his possessions before leaving for the forest exile, she persuaded her husband to go to the palace and narrate his plight to Rama. Trijata then related to Rama all his severe hardships, and Rama promised to give him all the cows residing within the distance up to which Trijata could throw his stick. There upon Trijata flung his stick with all his might across the Sarayu river and obtained a good number of cows.

Trijataa

An old rakshasi who, along with others, was assigned to guard Seeta confined in Ashokavana. When Seeta, in great despair, indicated that she wanted to kill herself, the rakshasi guardians expressed their delight in wanting to eat her flesh. At this stage, Trijataa narrated how she had dreamt of Rama destroying all the rakshasas of Lanka and retrieving his beloved wife. Hearing this Seeta regained her composure and awaited the early arrival of Rama.

Trishira

One of the sons of Ravana. He fought against Rama in Panchavati under the leadership of Khara. He was killed by Hanuman in the Lankan war.

Trunabindu

A rishi whose daughter Ilvila married Pulastya and gave birth to Paulastya, the father of Ravana.

U

Ulkamukha

A vanara chief who accompanied Angada, Hanuman and others during their search for Seeta in the southern direction.

Uma (Parvati)

Ganga and Parvati were the two daughters of Himalaya and Mena (Meru's daughter). When they came of age, Ganga was given in marriage to the devas and Uma undertook severe penances to get Shiva as her husband. This tale of early history was narrated by Vishvamitra to Rama and an assembly of munis when they were camping on the banks of Ganga. Rama was curious to know the origin of this holy river and Vishvamitra readily satisfied him.

Unmata

Son of rakshasa Malyavan and Sundari, daughter of gandharvi Narmada. Virupaksha and Durmukha were among his brothers and Anala was his sister.

Urmila

Mother of gandharvi Somada who served Chuli rishi very diligently and obtained from him a son who was named Brahmadatta. He married the hundred daughters of King Kushanabha. King Kushanabha then obtained, from a yagna, a son named Gadhi whose son was rishi Vishvamitra. This tale of ancestral history was narrated by rishi Vishvamitra to Rama and Lakshmana on their way to Mithila.

Urmila

Wife of Lakshmana. Daughter of King Janaka and sister of Seeta. Mother of Angada and Chitraketu.

Urvashi

In response to Lakshmana's query regarding the origin of the royal priest Vasishtha, Rama narrated a tale of early history according to which Vasishtha was born out of the seed of life of devas Mitra and Varuna which they had left in a pot when they encountered the divine apsara Urvashi.

V

Vaidarbhi

Wife of King Kusha and mother of Kushanabha who established the city of Mahodaya. Rishi Vishvamitra narrated the history of that area to Rama and Lakshmana while they were on their way to Mithila.

Vairochana

Father-in-law of Kumbhakarna — father of Vajrajwala.

Vaishravana (Kubera)

Brother of Ravana — son of Paulastya.

Vajradamshtra

A fierce rakshasa leader who, at the command of Ravana, went out with an army to fight against the vanara forces. Although he fought valiantly, he died at the hands of Angada in a prolonged battle.

Vajrajwala

Wife of Kumbhakarna — mother of Kumbha and Nikumbha.

Vajramulshi

A rakshasa leader who fought against the vanara forces in Lanka but was killed by Mainda vanara.

Vali

Vanara ruler of Kishkindha — elder brother of Sugreeva who served him faithfully. He was born out of an element of Indra.

Once Dundubhi, son of Mayasura, assuming the form of a buffalo, challenged Vali for a fight. After a prolonged battle Vali killed Dundubhi and flung his immense body to a distance of one yojana. In the process a few parts of Dundubhi's body fell into the ashram of Matanga rishi who then cursed Vali saying he would be killed if he ever stepped on the the premises of Rushyamuka mountain.

Later, Mayavi, elder brother of Dundubhi, came to the gate of Kishkindha and, itching for a fight, called out to Vali for a fight. Both Vali and Sugreeva came out. Seeing them Mayavi began to run and entered an underground cave. Vali followed him there and asked Sugreeva to guard the entrance of the cave. The fight between Vali and Mayavi went on for a very long time and there seemed to be no end. At last Sugreeva lost his patience and assuming that Vali had been killed, sealed the entrance to the cave and returned to the capital. But Vali who managed to slay Mayavi, found the entrance to the cave blocked. He suspected that Sugreeva had done this on purpose in order to usurp the Kingdom. Returning to the capital he then banished Sugreeva from the Kingdom. Sugreeva took refuge in Rushyamuka mountain along with Hanuman and other vanaras loyal to him.

In Rushyamuka he encountered Rama and Lakshmana and on the advice of Hanuman, he entered into a pact with Rama. Rama would kill Vali and crown Sugreeva as the King of Kishkindha and in return Sugreeva would find the whereabouts of Seeta.

Sugreeva then challenged Vali to a fight and as planned, Rama killed Vali by an arrow shot from behind a row of tree. Vali's wife Tara was then taken by Sugreeva and his son Angada was adopted by him.

Valmiki

Celebrated saint-poet of the Ramayana, famed as the Adi Kavi (first poet). In the early days of their forest exile, Rama, Lakshmana and Seeta encountered Valmiki rishi at his ashram in Chitrakoota mountain range. Later, they established their own abode in the same mountain range.

When Seeta was asked to depart from Ayodhya so that Rama could uphold public duty above personal happiness, she sought refuge in Valmiki rishi's ashram where she gave birth to twin sons, Lava and Kusha. Valmiki brought up the two boys and later took them to Ayodhya when Rama performed the ashwamedha yagna. There the two boys recited the Ramayana as taught by Valmiki.

Vamadeva

Vasishtha and Vamadeva were the two chief priests and counsellors of King Dasharatha of Ayodhya.

Varuni

Daughter of Varuna. She had emerged from the ocean churned by the devas and the asuras. She was accepted by the devas.

Vasishtha

One of the two royal priests of King Dasharatha; the other was Vamadeva. Vasishtha played a vital initial role in persuading King Dasharatha to send Rama with Vishvamitra to the forest to help the sage perform his yagna. Ironically, he was also once an antagonist of Vishvamitra. He established the supremacy of 'brahmic power'.

Vasishtha was the chief priest at the marriage of Rama and Seeta in Mithila. He had 'many brilliant and famous' sons engaged in austerities like their father. When King Trisanku sought their help to go to heaven in his bodily form, they refused as their father had done earlier. When the king threatened to seek other 'refuge', the sons of Vasishtha cursed him to turn into a chandala. As was the father, so were the sons in their power of 'tapas'.

Vasu

Youngest of the four sons of King Kosha and Queen Vaidarbhi. He established the city of Girivraja or Vasumati. This tale of early history was related by Vishvamitra rishi to Rama and Lakshmana while going through the forest.

Vasuda

Wife of rakshasa Mali – daughter of gandharvi Narmada – sister of Sundari (wife of Malyavana).

Vatapi

Vatapi and Ilvala were two cruel rakshasa brothers. Ilvala would often assume the form of a pious brahmana and invite various rishis. By previous arrangement, Vatapi would assume the form of a sacrificial goat. Ilvala would kill and cook the goat and feed the meat to the rishis. After consuming the meat Ilvala would call for Vatapi who would tear open the stomachs of the rishis and emerge outside. In this way the brothers killed many innocent rishis. Once Ilvala invited Agastya rishi and fed him goat meat as usual. But this time Vatapi was unable to come out because Agastya rishi by his yogic power had completely digested Vatapi. An angry Ilvala then rushed to kill Agastya but he was burnt to ashes by the mere glance of the great rishi. This tale was related by Vishvamitra rishi to Rama and Lakshmana as they went through the forest towards the ashram of Agastya rishi.

Vedavati

Granddaughter of guru Brahaspati. It was her father Kushadhwaja's desire that she should be married to Vishnu and to no one else. Coming to know of this, Shumbha, the King of daityas, got so angry that he killed Kushadhwaja while he was asleep. Vedavati then undertook severe penances in the Himalayas. It was there that Ravana happened to see her and, enamoured by her beauty, he asked her to marry him. Upon hearing her refusal, he forcibly pulled her and tried to catch her. Freeing herself from his grip she ended her life by entering into a raging fire. Before dying she proclaimed that she would return to the earth to demolish him. Thus it was that she was reborn in a later age as Seeta, the daughter of King Janaka.

Vegadarshi

A vanara chief who, along with Jambavan, Sushena and others, guarded the southern front when Rama arranged his army for battle against the Lankan rakshasas.

Vibhishana

Younger brother of Ravana and Kumbhakarna — son of rishi Vishravas and Kaikesi.

Along with his two brothers he had undertaken severe penances to please Brahma and had obtained an assurance that he would be helped to stick to the path of righteousness.

When Ravana kidnapped Seeta and brought her to Lanka, Vibhishana advised Ravana to return her to Rama and seek his forgiveness; this advice was ignored. Later, when Hanuman came to look for Seeta and was captured by the rakshasas, Ravana wanted him to be killed. But Vibhishana advised that, as Hanuman had come as an ambassador, he should not be killed but merely punished. Then, when Hanuman's tail was set aflame and released he jumped all over Lanka and burnt many buildings. Vibhishana's mansion remained unouched. Finally, when Ravana openly accused him of being the blacksheep of the family, he left his wife Sarma and daughter Kala behind and defected to Rama's side along with Anala, Panasa, Sampati and Pramati. Sugreeva and others viewed him with suspicion and wanted to kill him but Rama accepted him as an ally. Vibhishana then gave Rama valuable information about the rakshasa forces and their strategic locations. Rama then coronated him as the King of Lanka in exile. Before the battle of Lanka, when Shaka, Sarana and Shardool rakshasas came to Rama's camp in disguise, it was Vibhishana who recognized them and had them arrested. He advised

Rama in many other ways. In particular, he told him about the essential need to interrupt Indrajit's yagna of Nikumbhila devi which would otherwise have given him invincibility. When Indrajit's rakshasas began to fight Rama's forces by becoming invisible, it was once again Vibhishana who washed the eyes of Rama, Lakshmana and others with divine liquid obtained from Kubera so that they could see and fight the rakshasas who, otherwise, would have remained invisible. During the actual battle he killed many rakshasas. Finally, when Ravana was killed he was installed on the throne of Lanka.

He was present in Ayodhya at the coronation of Rama and attended Rama's ashwamedha yagna.

According to the puranas, he is one of the immortals (Chiranjeevi).

Vidyujiuha

Husband of Ravana's sister Surpanakha – father of Shambhu.

Vidyujivha

A rakshasa colleague of Ravana who, by witchcraft, made an artificial head of Rama which Ravana showed to Seeta in order to convince her that her husband had been killed and that therefore she should agree to become his Queen. This trick, however, did not work because, as soon as Ravana left Ashokavana, the artificial head also disappeared.

Vidyutakesha

Son of Heti, an early rakshasa. His wife was Salkantaka. He was the grandfather of Sumali rakshasa and great grandfather of Ravana's wife Kaikesi.

Vikta

One of the rakshasis ordered by Ravana in Ashokavana to try and persuade Seeta to yield to him.

Vinata

Another rakshasi who, along with Vikta, tried to persuade Seeta to accept Ravana as her husband.

Vinata

One of the leading commanders of the vanara sena. He led the mission to the east in search of Seeta and find out where Ravana had kept her captive.

Viradha

Once gandharva Tumbaru did not attend to Kubera who was in the company of apsara Rambha. Kubera cursed that Tumbaru turn into Viradha, a rakshasa. At Tumbaru's repeated pleadings, Kubera relented a little and said that he would regain his original form and return to swarga when he, as Viradha rakshasa, was killed by Rama and Lakshmana.

Viradha then undertook severe penances to please Brahma and obtained from him a boon by which he could not be killed by any weapon.

When Rama, Lakshmana and Seeta were crossing Dandakaranya forest, they encountered Viradha who wanted to possess Seeta. In the fight that ensued Viradha captured both Rama and Lakshmana. But they fought back and cut off both his arms. Knowing that he could not be killed by any weapon, they buried him in a deep pit. Viradha then regained his original form as Tumbaru gandharva and rose to heaven.

Virupaksha

A rakshasa leader who was asked by Ravana to guard the central front of the Lanka palace. In the fight with Rama's forces he was killed by Lakshmana.

Viryasaha

Son of King Saudasa, an early ancestor of Rama. After the death of his father, he ascended the throne under the name of Mitrasaha. Once, while his great ashwamedha yagna was coming to an end, a rakshasa recalling that his colleague had been killed by King Saudasa, came there in the guise of Vasishtha and requested that he be served a meat dish. King Mitrasaha gave instructions accordingly. In the meantime the rakshasa, assuming the guise of a royal cook, prepared a dish containing human flesh and the King served this dish to Vasishtha. Realising that the dish served to him, contained flesh, Vasishtha got angry and cursed that the King be turned into a rakshasa for a period of twelve years. The King, in turn, wanted to curse Vasishtha but was prevented by the Queen. King Mitrasaha then poured the specially prepared water on his own feet which instantly turned black. From then on he was known as Kalmashapada. This tale of early history was related by Valmiki to Shatrughna.

Vishal

Son of apsara Alambusha and King Ikshvaku, founder of the solar dynasty. He founded the city of Vishalanagari wherein Ahalya had remained lifeless and motionless like a stone due to the curse of her husband Gautama rishi. He was an early ancestor of Rama.

Vishravas (Paulastya)

Son of prajapati Pulastya and Trinabindu's daughter Ilvila. Vaishravana, better known as Kubera, was born as the son of Vishravas and Devavarnini, daughter of rishi Bharadwaja. Vishravas also accepted Sumali rakshasa's daughter Kaikesi who gave birth to Ravana, Kumbhakarna and Vibhishana. He also married Sumali's other daughter Raika who gave birth to Khara and Surpanakha.

Vishvamitra

Although born as a kshatriya king, he became a great rishi after realizing, in an encounter with rishi Vasishtha, that the spiritual strength of a brahmana was greater than the armed might of a kshatriya. Through intense studies, severe penances and austerities he became a rishi, then a rajarishi and ultimately a brahmarishi.

In the Ramayana, he appears at the court of Ayodhya and requests King Dasharatha to allow his teenage son Rama to accompany him to the forest to get rid of Marichi, Subahu and other rakshasas who were not allowing the rishis to complete their yagnas. Dasharatha was reluctant to send his young son Rama but agreed when the royal priest Vasishtha assured him that Rama would be safe.

Both Rama and Lakshmana then accompanied rishi Vishvamitra who gave them divine mantras and weapons and taught them the art of warfare. Eventually, Rama killed many rakshasas and the demoness Tataka and received blessings from the relieved rishis. Throughout their forest journey, Vishvamitra related the history of various places they passed. Then they met a band of travelling rishis who were proceeding to Janakapuri to attend the grand yagna being performed by King Janaka. They joined the group and reached Mithila where in a svayamvara Rama won the hand of Seeta. Vishvamitra narrated the greatness of King Dasharatha before Rama married Seeta.

Vishvakarma

Architect of the devas who, at the request of Indra, had built Lanka. At his suggestion the early rakshasas Malyavan, Sumali, Mali and others started living there.

Vrutasura

Towards the end of Rama's long and glorious rule, he had an idea of performing the Rajasuya yagna but Shatrughna voiced concern that many smaller rulers would come to grief. Rama accepted this view. At this juncture Lakshmana suggested that Ashwamedha yagna be conducted instead. In support of this argument Lakshmana then related the following tale from early history to underline the importance and power of Ashwamedha yagna.

Prajapati Tvashta's son Vishvarupa had been killed by Indra in earlier times. In order to avenge this heinous crime, Tvashta created Vrutasura to kill Indra. Though a daitya, Vrutasura ruled righteously over the earth. After a long rule he gave up his throne to his son Madhureshwara and went away to lead an austere life of penance. Coming to know of this and fearing that Vrutasura may obtain some great boon to overpower them, the devas went to Vishnu and requested him to kill Vrutasura. But Vishnu, citing his earlier treaty of friendship with Vrutasura, refused to kill him. Instead, he transferred one-third of his own power to Indra so that Indra himself could kill Vrutasura.

Indra went to the place where Vrutasura was sitting in deep meditation and without warning, beheaded him. As a result of this abominable crime Indra had to bear the sin of 'Brahmahatya'. When Indra thus became powerless, the whole world began to suffer. Finally, all the rishis got together and decided to perform an Ashwamedha yagna. On completion of this yagna, Brahmahatya dosha (the sin of homicide) left Indra's body and all was well once again. Such was the potency of Ashwamedha yagna.

Y

Yagnakopa

In one of the fiercest battles between rakshasas and vanaras on the outskirts of Lanka, Yagnakopa, along with fellow rakshasas Agniketu, Mitraghna and Rashmiketu, attacked Rama who beheaded all four of them with his burning arrows.

Yagnashatru

One of the twelve commanders of rakshasa Khara's army which fought against Rama in the forest.

Yuddhonamatta

A rakshasa chief whose palace was burnt down by Hanuman with his burning tail, as he jumped from one building to another in Lanka.

Yudhajita

Brother of Queen Kaikeyi. At the time of King Dasharatha's death, Bharata was visiting Yudhajita in Keikaya pradesh.

Yupaksha

A rakshasa who was killed by Hanuman during the battle between the forces of Rama and Ravana.